THE
SELF-DETERMINED
TEACHER

USING THE BEHAVIOR PRINCIPLES OF MOTIVATION TO RE-INSPIRE YOUR EDUCATIONAL FIRE

Anissa Moore, M.Ed., BCBA, LBA

For Sean and Sabrina

You are my biggest motivation, and the reason I strive to be my best self. We will forever be the "Three Musketeers" and I love you both with all my soul. Thank you for this beautiful life.

Table of Contents

PART I

WHEN DID WE LOSE OUR FIRE?

———————————•———————————

What inspired you to become an educator? Was there a little voice that told you, "I want to teach kids," or "I want to make a difference in students' lives," or even, "I want my summers off." (If you are laughing at this last statement because you know it's a lie, you are definitely in education!) Regardless of the reason, there was an overall drive to make a difference and change the world, one child at a time. This was the match that sparked your fire.

I didn't want to be a teacher when I was younger, or even when I started college. My mother was a master middle school English teacher who spent hours after school on curriculum committees, in department head meetings, and grading hundreds of papers each weekend. My father began as a teacher and later transitioned into the field of school finance and administration, serving for several years as an assistant superintendent in our hometown school district. He, too, spent multiple hours on weekends and over holidays attending district events, ball games, and even driving around campuses at 3 a.m. on freeze days to help determine if schools were going to be closed due to icy roads. I remember that some days I was very popular with my friends when those decisions were made, and on other days, I wasn't. My grandmother was a retired teacher. I had aunts who were teachers, cousins who were teachers, and my other grandmother was a school cafeteria manager before she retired, and one of my aunts took over. Educators surrounded me, and it was just our way of life.

I couldn't wait to leave my mid-size Texas town and do something different. Something big. Something that was uniquely me. I earned an academic scholarship to attend a small university in New Mexico, where I planned to study anthropology and archaeology. I was ready to be the next female Indiana Jones. I had a fire. I wanted to travel the world, study different cultures, and experience new things. I left Texas to attend my first year of college and discovered very quickly that Indiana Jones was a MOVIE.

In one of my classes, we were taken to an empty stretch of land in the middle of nowhere in New Mexico and were each assigned a 6x6 plot of land to analyze. We were given a data sheet, a clipboard, a pencil, and a medium-sized paintbrush. We were instructed to swipe, swipe, swipe the dirt with the paintbrush and then record any artifacts or non-organic findings on our data sheet. Why didn't we dig, you may be asking? Because that disturbs the land too abruptly and could damage a potential "find." So, twice a week, I diligently swiped specific sections of my assigned land and recorded my findings. There's a beer bottle cap, record it. There's a lipstick-stained cigarette butt — eww — record it. As my fire dwindled down and slowly began to burn out, all I could think was, "Indiana Jones probably never did this."

You see, motivation for what we do on a day-to-day basis is critical to our well-being. If we don't have a fire (even if it's a small one at times), then we start to lose interest in our efforts and outcomes. We begin to go through the motions of the day, losing a drive to educate while losing a small part of ourselves at the same time. I wrote this book for you, your teammates, the staff you lead, and the students you mentor and inspire every day. I wrote this book for that inner first-year teacher or administrator that's still in you, the one who still wants to make a lasting impact. But I also wrote it for myself, for my educational colleagues and leaders who have catalyzed my success, and for my family, who motivates me to dream big every day.

As you read each chapter, keep in mind that motivation doesn't instantly come to us. Instead, it is a set of behaviors we can establish and improve upon, and those behaviors are like matches that you can strike whenever you need a little fire. I also want you to know that this book is not a "hard read"; you have enough of that to do in educational research, curriculum reviews, and assessment results. Instead, this book is a tool for you. A guide to grab when you need it. Your matchbox.

Anissa Moore

Chapter 1

The Magnitude
of Motivation: My Story

———————•———————

Have you ever been in a season of your life in which you had no drive, no motivation, no FIRE? If so, you know it's a tough season to weather. So there I was, away at college, feeling lost and unsure of my future. Although I loved my university, my dear Chi Omega sisters I had gained, and the gorgeous New Mexico seasons, I missed Texas. I missed my family. I ventured back to Texas and settled in San Antonio (a large but friendly city that to this day is the perfect fit for me). I started attending college in San Antonio without much of a plan, and without so much as a match to light any fire I was searching for. I decided to major in English (like my mom), not because I knew what I wanted to do, but simply because I was good at it, and I loved to write. I had a passion for writing since I could pick up a pencil, earning school awards and having poems published in local magazines and campus publications, but it wasn't something I wanted to pursue as a career. The thought of being told what to write and how to write from a supervisor or publishing house sounded very unappealing. I drifted through college, operating on autopilot—disconnected, uninspired.

After I completed my second year of college, I went to both of my parents (who were divorced by this time, but *very* much on the same page with how they valued and viewed a college education!) and said, "I think I need to take a break from school. I don't know what I want to do with my life, and I feel like I need to go find myself." I did not win any daughter points for this, but my family supported my decision to "find" myself, as long as I could "find" myself a job and "find" a way to take care of the bills. So off I went in search of my fire.

I had some interest in becoming a lawyer, so I took a job at an attorney's office that was very short-lived. The attorney was an angry, mean-spirited man who belittled his staff, including his wife (who was his bookkeeper). The toxic work environment quickly disillusioned me and soured my interest in pursuing a career in law. I returned to retail, which I had been very successful at in high school, but only to make a living. I loved working with customers and the "social butterfly" aspect of retail, but the hours were erratic and the pay was low. My father kept encouraging me, "Why don't you look at something in education?" I think my response was, "That's y'all's thing, not my thing," but in my mind I said, "Over my dead body – I want to be different." My father always used to say, "The best-kept secret in education is being a librarian." He would talk about how the interactions with students were less stressful than teaching in the classroom, and with my love of reading and writing, he thought it would be a good fit. I was somewhat intrigued but not yet motivated to make a move in that direction. After living hand-to-mouth for several months working two jobs and growing tired of eating 50-cent ramen noodles, I reluctantly applied for a computer aide position at a middle school down the street from my apartment. My thought was that this may suffice for a bit, get me some insurance, and allow me weekends off to supplement my income at my second job at a video store. Here's a blast from the past: does anyone remember *Blockbuster Video*? Please be kind and rewind…because I was the gal who had to rewind all the VHS tapes before restocking them. All…of…them.

I was contacted for an interview at the middle school and walked in ready to assume this computer aide position was just a temporary gig until I found my fire. I met the principal - a kind, welcoming man with an easy demeanor - who made me feel comfortable right away. We briefly discussed the interview questions before he took off his glasses, sat back, and looked at me. "I have a feeling about you."

What does that mean? I thought. Am I screwing this up already? He continued to say, "I know you came in for the computer aide position, but I want to talk with you about another open position. This would be an instructional aide in a special education classroom." Special ed? I didn't know much about special needs, but I asked to hear more about the position. I would be assigned to a life skills classroom supporting students with significant cognitive disabilities, working closely with the special education teacher. My principal seemed to pick up on my hesitation, so he said, "I can show you the classroom, and I can send you to some training this summer before you start." (Personal note: paraprofessional training is critical, and if you're an administrator who sends your paras to training, I'm giving you a gold star!) I agreed to see the classroom, then accepted the position without truly knowing what I was getting into.

Summer training came and went, and I learned about various disabilities, developmental delays, speech and communication, and behavior supports. It was a whirlwind three days, but after the first day, I felt inspired. I was downright pumped! I had a new curiosity I hadn't felt since high school, and that dormant fire was rekindled. My teacher and I started the first week of school with about eight 6th-8th graders with autism, Down Syndrome, cerebral palsy, and other developmental disabilities. I had a student in a wheelchair, two students in pull-ups, and one who was completely nonverbal and bit his hand when he got excited, happy, anxious, or angry (he was an equal-opportunity biter). I diapered, I fed, I read, I taught, I modeled skills, and I practiced using proactive behavior supports with escalating students... and I loved every minute of it.

Back then, I made about $800 a month after taxes and insurance, and I still loved it. Anyone who's been in education knows that one does not go into the field – or remain in the field – for the money, since it's so little. I realized I was motivated to be there because of the students and how I felt when I was supporting them. As soon as my students got on the bus each day, I walked across the street and worked in the toddler room at a daycare until 6:30 every night. I continued to work at Blockbuster Video every weekend to pay the bills and eat more than ramen. Juggling three jobs was exhausting, but it was worth it just to be immersed in an environment where I felt helpful, loved, and appreciated. The climate at my middle school was usually fun and upbeat. Things were falling into place for me, quite accidentally. I finished the school year, but I knew what I needed to do next: high-tail it back to college and get my teaching certification. The very path I had once dismissed became the one calling I couldn't ignore: match - spark - fire - purpose. However, I forever remain that I DID do something different than my family, since no one was in special education. I'm counting it!

Now, over 30 years later, I've been promoted to specialist, special education coordinator, assistant director, college teacher, Board Certified Behavior Analyst, and now an independent consultant — and I've loved it all. I still do. But nothing comes easy; I still have to work at it each day. Each day, I try to find the good because it doesn't always find me. Each day, I have to take some deep breaths and pause, if only for a moment, to take it all in and juggle the challenges with the triumphs. As a behavior analyst, I've learned acceptance and commitment therapy techniques that help me implement small daily activities to sustain my motivation (which I will pass along to you). As a parent, I've learned the critical need for patience. As a lifelong educator, I have learned that kindling the motivational fire is a set of actions I must take. To be successful and happy, these actions come with the job. Hence, the birth of this book.

The magnitude of motivation in our careers is immeasurable; it's what gets us up in the morning, keeps us working, and keeps us content. Motivation is directly linked to a growth mindset, those two educational buzzwords that encourage us to continue learning, thinking, and growing in our day-to-day lives. It's what keeps us from getting stuck and getting stagnant. What I want you to keep in your mind and your heart for the rest of this book is that:

1) motivation is not an automatic emotion that is just handed to us, but a feeling of purpose that has to be created, practiced, and sustained through consistent behaviors, and

2) Motivation doesn't guarantee perfect days of sunshine and happiness, but should be viewed as that inner fire that fuels your commitment each day to show up and keep going, even when faced with challenges and adversity

Motivation is a skill set; it's a daily practice. It's work, but it's SO worth it. Your students are worth it. YOU are worth it. You are worth the work. The fact that you even picked up this book to read shows that you still have a light left in you that wants to stay bright. You still have a desire to give your all to your job. You're not done…. far from it.

You're just getting started.

Chapter 2

What is
Self-Determination?

———————•———————

Try to picture what you look like and feel like when you feel determined to do something. You may feel your pulse racing a little more, or have a small rush of adrenaline, or hear an inner voice that says, "Do this. Now." Feeling self-determined means having the freedom to make your own choices. Self-determination means you have control over your own life and your own destiny, and you act accordingly.

Self-determination theory (SDT) is the belief that human motivation, or in this case, teacher motivation, is guided by the drive to fulfill our basic psychological needs for autonomy, competence, and relatedness. Self-determination theory was developed by psychologists Edward Deci and Richard Ryan in their initial book, *Self-Determination and Intrinsic Motivation in Human Behavior* (1985).

Self-Determination Theory - breaking down our psychological needs:

• Autonomy refers to having a choice in one's behaviors; the feeling of having some input, control, and options in our work (ex. what materials to use when teaching a concept, your leadership strategies and presentation style).

• Competence refers to having understanding and confidence in both your subject matter and what is being asked of you in your role. Educators feel competent when they know their behaviors are effective and meet or exceed the standards set for them.

• Relatedness refers to the feeling of belonging, closeness, and support that one experiences with others. In educational settings, relatedness is fostered when educators feel connected, both intellectually and emotionally, to their peers and to their campus or district climate.

The research suggests that when these needs are met, our motivation not only peaks but also becomes more deeply rooted and self-driven. Now, if you've worked in a school system for more than a year, you know that there are always guidelines and expectations that must be followed as outlined in your policies. There's no way around that, and believe it or not, those policies are in place to set high expectations for students and to ensure continuity across campuses and staff. You may not have complete autonomy in everything you do, teach, or respond to. Still, there are so many other ways to grow the independence, competence, and relatedness that you have in the areas you teach and lead every single day.

When thinking about the connections you have with students, colleagues, and your work environment, how do you rate yourself? Consider the following to help you determine areas you have more self-determination and areas that may be a focus for growth:

- I have autonomy (or can provide input) in my lessons, leadership, and/or supplemental instructional materials

- I feel confident and competent in my subject matter and administrative abilities, and in how I relay it to students

- I collaborate with teammates and like-minded peers regularly

- I seek out additional ideas on my own accord

- When I experience challenges, I solicit support from other peers/leadership/resources/self-research

- I genuinely like teaching/educating/leading in my field and still find it interesting

- I think what I am doing is important and relevant

Now, look at your answers and take a minute to reflect on each response. Where are some areas where you see a pattern of more self-determination, and where are some places that you feel like you're struggling?

Stronger area(s):

_____

_____

_____

Challenging area(s):

_____

_____

_____

We'll use some of these responses in a later chapter.

When you identify challenges to your self-determination, think more deeply: are there any variables within your control that you can change? If so, what are they?

_____

_____

_____

_____

_____

_____

Some of the most challenging "work" I'll ask you to do is to not only identify areas that may be within your capacity to improve upon, but to approach these challenges with optimism. When you are optimistic about an upcoming challenge, project, or change in your life, you will be amazed at what you can accomplish.

Chapter 3

The Research Behind Optimism

---•---

One of my favorite movies of all time is the Reese Witherspoon classic, *Legally Blonde* (MGM, 2001). It's one of those movies I've seen a hundred times, yet whenever it's on TV I find myself watching it again. After studying the theory of self-determination and the theory of optimism, I realized that I'm continuously drawn to this movie for one main reason: the character's unwavering optimism. The character of "Elle Woods", played by Witherspoon, decides to win the love of her life back by applying to Harvard law school (where he is attending). She meets with her college counselor who asks, "What are your backups?", to which she replies, "I don't need backups. I'm going to Harvard." Shortly after this scene, Elle is studying for her LSAT exam when her best friends come into her room to see what she is doing. Elle excitedly answers, "Girls, I'm going to Harvard!" No doubt, no fear, just optimism…and some hard work. Even during challenges and some tears throughout her journey, the character remains self-determined until the end. You see, optimism doesn't guarantee a happy ending, but it encourages our mindset that it is possible and attainable.

A substantial body of research supports the theory of optimism in work and in life. Whether it be rooting for an underdog in a movie, cheering for a positive coworker who is fighting a personal challenge, or harnessing our own optimism, as a society we tend to gravitate toward optimistic outcomes. Now, many people think that an optimistic person is someone who is happy-go-lucky all the time, skipping along a rainbow-sprinkled path, never thinking that anything will go wrong. In reality, this is not true at all. Optimism is the belief that even if things are going wrong, they can still improve. Optimism is the belief that we are not stuck; we are just paused for a little bit in our challenge until we summon the drive to keep going. Again, the practice of optimism is work, but it is a practice that will pay off in everything you do, every day. Believe me, I know.

The year 2007 was both the most fantastic and the worst year of my life. I was pregnant with our first and only child. I worked as a school district administrator and loved both my team and my supervisors. I had just passed my board exams to become a certified behavior analyst. And to top it all off, we were preparing to move into the brand-new home we had built for our growing family. It was a big year of changes, and I was filled with excitement, fire, and yes – optimism.

It was the end of September, and we had just closed on our new home with our baby girl, who was just a few months old. I was still drained and exhausted from having a C-section, and shortly after, I developed pneumonia. I was mourning the loss of my ability to breast-feed my sweet baby girl. After giving birth, I worked with a lactation consultant and she and my doctor deemed I was one of the very few that were unable to actually produce milk to feed my little girl. I remember being so confused because I had read all the books, done the classes, and researched all of the techniques (in typical behavior analyst form!) A lot of emotions were high, yet I had amazing friends and family who came to help us move into our new home. When I went to our family doctor and discovered I had pneumonia, I had mentioned something that the lactation nurse had mentioned to me in the hospital… I had a complex round area in my left breast that our baby could not get around, and it was causing me not to produce milk. As much as I hated getting pneumonia, ironically, it saved my life.

My family doctor, who at that time was about the same age as me, said that he wanted to send me for a diagnostic mammogram to "be on the safe side ". He reassured me that I was young and it was likely nothing, but he didn't want to take any chances. Given my age at the time, it took a couple of months for our insurance to approve the request, but once they did, it became a whirlwind from then on. We closed on our house the last week of September and started packing. By the end of that week, I had my first mammogram as an early 30-something year-old. We moved into our new home that weekend, trying not to think of anything else but unpacking and getting our baby settled. We were told it could take up to a week to get the results, but then the phone rang on Monday morning. It was the doctor's office, saying they wanted me to come in that afternoon and bring my husband with me. My husband and I entered the waiting room, not sure what we were actually waiting for.

"We need to run some more tests so that we can stage you, but right now it's looking like stage three." The doctor was kind but direct. "Stage three?" I repeated out loud. "What?" I became a zombie after that, not sure if I had heard correctly. "Like it's breast cancer?" Looking back now, as I relive that moment, I think, what a dumb question to ask since they had done a breast mammogram and I was in an oncology office. Still, you know we all tend to say stupid or unusual or shocking things when we have a thousand emotions going on. Ironically, this day was October 1st, which historically kicks off breast cancer awareness month.

The irony was not lost on us. I was referred to yet another oncologist who was strong, dynamic, and looked like a supermodel. She was stunning, reassuring, and looked me dead in the eyes, and said, "You are not going to die, and you will get through this." Talk about a bedside manner! That is the classic example of optimism. She wasn't dancing around, pretending that everything was OK right now, but she was square-faced, telling me that it would be OK after we went through all the things we needed to do. In other words, we needed to do some work.

Now, I don't want you to play the comparison game and think that any physical, emotional, or mental challenges you might be going through right now are less significant than something like a cancer diagnosis, because everyone's story is different. Everyone's battle is as distinct and unique as their fingerprint. And every battle is relevant. There is no shame in being upset or frustrated over daily events, such as your students calling you the "B" word or receiving another email from one of those parents who constantly complain, never satisfied with your efforts. Your struggle is your own, and don't ever let anyone minimize your feelings.

However, what I want you to do through the use of this book and its daily practices is to work on the behavior of optimism. I'll be providing you with brief, easy-to-implement ideas that can not only increase your self-determination but also help you recognize pessimistic statements and reframe them into optimistic ones. You will be amazed at the changes that you feel over time. Remember, the residual effects that you start to see far exceed the impact in your classroom or with your students and coworkers. Optimism will have a positive effect on so many other areas of your life, too.

Ready…. (mind)set…. go!

PART II

LET'S GET TO WORK

———————•———————

Simple Daily Practices and Purposeful

Actions to Light Your Educational Fire (Again!)

Chapter 4

Mindset Then Skill Set

————————●————————

Before applying daily or weekly practices that can improve your overall motivation to continue in education, you must first adopt a growth mindset. Otherwise, you'll approach this book half-heartedly and not reap the benefits I intend to provide you with. Remember, this book is for YOU. You sought it out because a little voice told you that you could gain support and stamina for what you were born to do.

Let's suppose you've been in education for a while. In that case, you've probably been trained in teaching your students about their growth mindset: how to recognize a growth mindset from a fixed mindset, ways to identify fixed-mindset thinking and statements, and how to build a growth mindset in the classroom and with tasks. But let me ask you honestly: do you practice what you teach? A growth mindset keeps our minds from getting stuck and becoming stale. Our mindsets remind us every day how to accept obstacles and react to them with a planned outcome of learning something from each obstacle. A growth mindset doesn't guarantee positive outcomes all the time, but similar to optimism, it helps us understand that there are possibilities for growth and change.

I'd like you to write a simple, uncomplicated growth mindset statement to prepare your brain for the strategies to follow. If you need help getting started, there are some sentence stems below:

My mindset statement:

_____

_____

_____

_____

_____

Here are a few examples if you need some sentence starters:

One thing I wish I could change about my current situation to make it more positive is…...

_____

_____

_____

_____

_____

_____

_____

_____

When thinking about where I want my career motivation to be, I hope that ......

_____

_____

_____

_____

_____

_____

_____

_____

_____

After considering where I'm currently at in my work attitude, I want to take steps to become ......

_____

_____

_____

_____

_____

_____

_____

_____

_____

_____

Chapter 5

Write Your Why: Why Did You Become an Educator in the First Place?

─────────●─────────

I remember when I first became a district-level administrator, we would participate in various book studies each year as a leadership team. One year we read Simon Sinek's *Start with Why* (2009). I loved this book because it emphasized the importance of a growth mindset— both for my evolving career and my current team. It also reignited my passion and reminded me of my "why." Although a big focus of Sinek's book is to help readers foster trust and community among clients and stakeholders, educators can use these principles to support being a more self-determined teacher by 1) identifying their own "why", 2) aligning teaching methods or leadership skills to their "why", and 3) modeling their own "why" for coworkers and students needing increased motivation. Taking this same approach, think about the initial reason that you became an educator: can you define your "why" based on the variables, events, or activities that got you here? Try to identify and write down your original "why":

Why did I originally become an educator/administrator / educational leader?

_____

_____

_____

_____

What were the specific events in my life and variables that contributed to my "why?"

_____

_____

_____

_____

Psychological research suggests that labeling your specific feelings can help you better address and cope with them. This psychological concept is often called "affect labeling", or the act of putting your emotions into words. Decades of research in neuroscience and psychology have shown that labeling your feelings can reduce their intensity and improve emotional regulation, making it easier to cope with them effectively and, in turn, self-regulate. For example, suppose you can define your feelings and actions when you are feeling happy, satisfied, or content. In that case, you can gain a better understanding of what motivates you professionally and thus calls upon those actions when needed at other times. Alternatively, by being able to identify and name the emotions tied to burnout and dissatisfaction, you can better take action to deal with those feelings through pre-taught coping strategies. And that, my friend, is what this book will help you find.

One of the areas of behavior analysis I have studied for years is Acceptance and Commitment Therapy. Acceptance and Commitment Therapy, or ACT, is a type of therapy that helps people accept complex thoughts and feelings instead of fighting them, stay present in the moment (more of this to come in a future chapter!), and take action toward dealing with those feelings as guided by their core values. However, it's challenging to take action based on your core values if you can't specifically identify them. In the following chapters, I will not be providing you with therapy; however, I will guide you through the process of identifying your values, developing self-regulation and coping strategies, and finding your fun again in your career.

Chapter 6

Recognizing Your Burnout

———————•———————

One of the most effective ways to help ourselves in challenging situations is to also identify the "why": why this challenge occurred, why did we react a certain way, and why it may have been unproductive. Labeling and defining the "good" and the "bad" can help us identify areas for self-improvement. Doing this self-reflection activity can help you narrow down what you want to change, improve, or strive for in creating your motivational career goals. It's challenging to set a professional goal to achieve if you don't know where your burnout lies.

Picture this: you have a beautiful-looking car. It's your favorite color. It smells amazing. It features the best cup holders for your 50-gallon water jug, which you lug to work every day. You love this car and you're thankful to have it, but there's one problem: the engine doesn't work. So, you can't go anywhere, even though you want to. If only the engine ran, everything else you love about your beautiful car would come together, and you'd be ready to roll. You love everything else about your car, but the one identified challenge masks all the positive things and stops you in your tracks.

Now picture your life, your educational career, and all the things you love about your job. Think about your leaders, your coworkers, your students, or the subject/grade you teach. Even think about other positives such as your short commute, or that custodian you work with who's always eager to help you carry things to your car, or if your own kids conveniently attend the district where you work. Picture those things that make the hard days tolerable. Better yet, since seeing is believing and believing is achieving, write down at least three things you love about your job so you can see them staring back at you as a visual reminder of the good stuff:

1. _____

_____

2. _____

_____

3. _____

_____

Now, back to that car you visualized that didn't have a working engine. How did your dream car stop working? What stopped the engine? If you could only figure that out, you could formulate a plan for repairing it. You wouldn't keep such a lovely car and never get it fixed, right? Here's where we address the root cause of your burnout; in other words, when your own engine stopped running.

Pinpointing the exact time or event that burned you out in your field is pretty tricky for most people, as burnout is 1) hard to measure objectively, and 2) is usually a series of events or moments that add up over time, challenging our motivation and our resilience. Returning to the lighting-a-match analogy - those symbolic sparks we're always trying to ignite - burnout happens when there's too much water dumped on our fire, repeatedly, before we have time to find another match to rekindle the flame. Ever felt that way? I certainly have, and that water not only dampened my fire, but some days I felt like I was drowning.

My first year as a school district administrator was *that* year. I was promoted from lead specialist on the autism team to special education coordinator for the district, and I was thrilled. I was pumped. My fire was lit. I was in my mid-30s, but I was determined to hold my own against my more seasoned team of coordinators and directors. After all, I had made it through chemo, surgeries, and radiation therapy, so this was a welcome challenge. I wasn't quite in remission yet, but definitely over the mountain, so I jumped into my leadership role with the determination to support campuses, staff, and their students with optimism as my co-pilot.

I began going into the office early to get a jump-start on the day. I gave principals my personal cell number with a "call me anytime" attitude.

And they did. Teachers would email me and ask, "Can you let me know [insert answer to any and every problem] by today if possible?" And I did. I got texts in the evenings from various coworkers, and I immediately responded. I wanted to be accessible, relatable, and helpful. On the inside, though, I wanted to prove my own worth. I would sing my daughter to sleep at night and then get into bed with my laptop (much to my husband's dismay), answering emails until my eyes got droopy and my brain couldn't function…only to wake up and head to the office early again. I quickly started to drown.

Family members and friends began telling me to "slow down" and take care of my body, but the challenge I faced was the precedent that was already set. Guess who set it? Yup, me. And once that precedent was set, it was hard to backtrack and slow down without looking like I was starting to slack off. The funny thing about wanting to be overly accessible to others is that you become excessively accessible. I was drowning, but I had pushed myself into that pool. No one was asking me to be this way, but I was. The light was burning out quickly in a year that started on fire.

I had to make some changes. I finished out the school year and took my three weeks off in the summer to spend with our daughter, who was just a few years old. Money was tight due to my medical bills, so we hadn't planned any trips. No fancy vacation, no big house projects, and no cleaning out closets - just playtime with my kid. We had tea parties, watched Sesame Street, went to the neighborhood pool, and took naps on the couch together. My husband and I resumed our dance parties in the kitchen as we cooked dinner. It was my life, and it was precious.

Reducing my self-imposed 60-hour workweek to a more manageable pace allowed me the time to reflect on my burnout. Since I had created this stress myself, I had the power to create compromises. I made a T-chart (once a teacher, always a teacher!) On the left side, I listed all the things I loved about my leadership role: my director and superintendent were kind and knowledgeable, my campuses respected me, my coworkers were collaborative and caring, and we lived in the school district where I worked. Then on the right side of the T-chart, I listed the things that were burning me out: excessive email responses, early mornings, late nights, and over-committing to projects. I realized that everything on that chart that was burning me out was something I had some autonomy over, and every positive aspect came from my connection with others. The happiness I experienced in my career didn't come from my job duties; it came from the connections I made. People were my business, and connecting with them made me a better leader, mom, and wife, because I was happy.

Your turn: go back and look at that list you created about the things you love about your job. Now, create a T-chart and see if you can identify specific aspects of your burnout.

Areas of Value   Areas of Burnout

Chapter 7

**Starting Strong
with One Intentional Goal**

———————•———————

Now that you have your mindset in a "ready to learn" mode, let me ask you…what was your hope in reading this book? Did you have a goal in mind when you decided to read (or listen to) the words on the pages? If you did, what was it? Write it down right here:

_____

_____

_____

If you didn't have a specific goal or driving force when you picked up this book, stop and pause a minute. Were you hoping to be reinspired in your subject area or leadership position? Were you hoping to overcome daily stressors to finish strong toward retirement? Maybe you were hoping to re-ignite your fire in order to promote and move forward with your educational career? Think of one specific, measurable goal that you hope to achieve after reading this book. Write it in a manner that reinforces the actual occurrence of your goal. Avoid statements like "I hope" or "I wish"; instead, use statements like "I will" or "This will" and write it with determination here:

_____

_____

_____

Now, grab an index card, a sticky note, or one of those cute little notepad pages that teachers tend to have on their desks or in their kitchens, and rewrite that goal. Keep that small note and put it somewhere you can see daily. This may be taped to the bottom of your keyboard at work, clipped on the visor of your car, or attached to your bathroom mirror. Finally, READ IT DAILY...yep, every day. There is incredible research behind visual cues and their impact on the brain. Setting a specific, intentional goal each day influences not only our thinking but also our actions. We'll dive deeper into the power of visual supports in the next chapter.

Chapter 8

The Power of the Picture

———————•———————

Visual cues, such as pictures, quotes, photos, and written words, can play a significant role in influencing motivation and optimism. For example, visual cues support our mental imagery; mental imagery activates many of the same neural pathways as actual performance. This allows our brain to rehearse success mentally and prepares us to take action with confidence. A study by Taylor et al. (1998) found that individuals who practiced positive visualization (i.e., imagining themselves achieving a goal) showed increased motivation and were more likely to engage in goal-directed behavior. Consider this: have you ever had a personal goal that you wanted to achieve, such as running a race, organizing your closets, or learning a new technology skill? When you think about that goal, are you watching videos online, reading articles, looking up pictures, or buying books about that ultimate goal? You're in education, so you're probably doing some research to help you obtain the knowledge and skills to help you accomplish that goal. Now think about *how* you research: are you watching videos of people training to run a race and then completing it? Are you browsing online pictures of professional organizers who have transformed a space to make it beautiful? These are the things that inspire you, right? You're seeing the end result, and it's helping you paint a picture of your own end result. Think about it: we're less likely to buy a marathon book with a cover showing a sweaty, struggling runner in pain than one with a strong, confident athlete nearing the finish line. We like *seeing* the possibilities, the triumph, the finish line. We enjoy seeing achievements because they prompt our mental imagery of our own potential and optimistic outcome. As the older-than-time saying goes, "seeing is believing."

The following several sections will provide you with simple, easy-to-implement strategies to encourage positive visualization, thus adding to your matchbox of motivation.

Chapter 9

The Sticky-Note Strategy

——————•——————

I love, love, love sticky notes! I have them everywhere, I use them for everything, and I have every color. Obsessed? Maybe a little….

However, sticky notes are incredibly versatile and can serve as a quick visual strategy when needed. As an educator or administrator, you likely have sticky notes within reach, making them a convenient tool in a time pinch (and as educators, aren't we *always* in a time pinch?) The simple act of writing down a thought, a phrase, or an encouraging word sends a signal to our brain to retain that written text, even in the short term. Writing notes to yourself — especially motivational ones, such as sticky notes with affirmations or goals — may seem insignificant. However, a substantial body of psychological and neuroscientific research supports the effectiveness of this technique in boosting motivation, self-regulation, and goal adherence.

When we write something like a daily goal or encouraging thought, we're translating that internal goal into an external visual cue that prompts and directs our behavior. What we've written becomes a visual support, a permanent product of our thought. Most adults use sticky notes to remind themselves to do something like buy a few groceries, call someone, or flag a page in a book with a key point they want to remember. I do this too, but a couple of years before COVID, I began expanding my use of these revolutionary little squares…quite by accident.

I was coaching in a Kindergarten classroom with an excellent-but completely fried-teacher. She had a student who was tearing up the room, demonstrating physical aggression toward peers and exhibiting a lot of work refusal behavior. The student was sharp as a tack, and the team hoped to keep him in his general education class as much as possible to maintain his academic rigor.

However, the teacher was exhausted each day from the energy this student required of her. Think about it: great teachers try to develop great methods and great strategies, which can equal great fatigue. This teacher was drained. I observed the student for a while and then met with the teacher during her conference time while the kids were out of the room. I was about to discuss some immediate ideas to implement for this student, when I saw the teacher's shoulders droop and her eyes become moist. At that moment, I knew that she couldn't fully take in any more "to-dos" that I was about to offer.

Does this sound like a familiar scenario to you? Can you relate? I know I can. I've had those moments, both as a teacher and an administrator, that have made me want to crawl into bed when I got home and call in sick the next day. This is normal, and it's the kind of scenario that calls for additional ideas of optimism and mindset *before* focusing on the skill set and "to-dos". The notion of "Maslow-before-Bloom", such as meeting students' basic needs before challenging them with higher-level thinking, is true for us too. If you are an educational coach or consultant, consider this notion the next time you encounter the completely drained educator you're coaching. I promise if you provide just a few minutes of emotional check-in and listening empathy, in turn you will get a more willing, more open-to-ideas educator.

I read the teacher's face and told her, "Before we get started, I want to hear your take on the toughest behavior we need to tackle first. Do you have a sticky note I can use?" The teacher nodded and motioned to her desk. I intended to write down the one "big" behavior interference as a visual focus, then draw an arrow pointing to the right with an appropriate replacement behavior that we would brainstorm. I often used this technique to encourage one thing at a time — one behavior at a time — and it is usually short but powerful. However, when I reached the teacher's desk, I saw three or four sticky-note pads in various colors and sizes. One of them was a white sticky pad with a small picture of *Winnie the Pooh* at the top, right by a quote from his boy-buddy Christopher Robin that said, "You are braver than you believe, stronger than you seem, and smarter than you think." I had seen or heard the quote many times, being a big "Pooh" fan myself, but on this day, it hit me like a ton of bricks. I took a page from that particular pad and sat down beside the teacher, and said, "I love this sticky notepad! Where did you get it?" She told me that it was a gift from a student before the holiday break. I then said, "This is great. Now, can you read this for me?" She looked a little confused (more like she thought I was crazy), but after a pause, she read it softly out loud. "Thank you," I replied. "Now, can you reread it, like you believe it? The student who gave it to you believes it." She laughed at me a little through tears and repeated the quote — half humoring me, half absorbing the words — as she sat up a little straighter in her chair. Then I took the sticky note back from her and wrote one word immediately under the Christopher Robin quote before returning it to her. That word was BELIEVE. I reminded her (and myself in that moment) that she needed to believe that this situation was approachable, achievable, and worth the work. A few days later, when I returned to her room to drop off some behavior visuals, I saw that sticky note taped to the right of her mousepad on her laptop. Right in her daily line of sight.

From that moment on, I felt the true impact of visual words and phrases on our mood and mindset. I started coaching teachers to grab a sticky note off their desk and write down a word, phrase, or sentence that made them feel strong; something that made them feel special as an educator. Then I had them put the sticky note in a place they could see it every day, such as the corner of their computer monitor or keyboard, taped on top of their classroom phone, or somewhere on their desk. Something as simple as a sticky note that you write to yourself can become a daily mindset reminder. Don't underestimate the power of simplicity; quick strategies are easier to implement for busy educators but can still pack an evidence-based punch. This book of "matches" I've written for you is filled with evidence-based simplicity!

Digging a little deeper into the science behind this simple strategy, research on the "generation effect" (Slamecka & Graf, 1978) reveals that people tend to remember and value content they generate themselves more than content that is presented to them. Writing your notes or mantras personalizes the message, which increases the likelihood that your brain will pay attention to and act on it. A sticky note in your workspace serves as a tiny, environmental "nudge", reinforcing attention and intention every time it is seen.

If you have access to a sticky note right now, what would you write on it? Is there a word or a phrase that resonates with you and makes you feel just a little more empowered after you read it? Now write it down and place it in a visible location where you can see it daily. If you don't have a sticky note handy, stop reading for just a few minutes and find one. Go on…. I'll wait.

Insert your
awesomeness
here.

Chapter 10

What's Your Mantra?

───────●───────

For thousands of years, people have believed in the power of a mantra. This daily saying, repeated over and over, goes from short- term memory to long-term memory. In other words, it becomes ingrained. It becomes habitual and thus is easy to retrieve whenever you need to call upon it. Research has shown that mantras influence self- perception, stress regulation, and goal-directed behavior, all of which enhance motivation and optimism. Raise your hand if you need help with stress! When we are stressed, overworked, or overtired (basically, when we are being educators), it becomes harder for us to think as sharply as we do when we are not in a state of stress. Having a simple, habitual phrase that requires little cognitive effort to recall can ground us during moments of overwhelm. Regular repetition of mantras may downregulate activity in the amygdala (the stress center of our brain), increasing emotional regulation and mental clarity. More and more teachers and administrators have reported to me that difficulty with emotional regulation of students has a direct impact on their own emotional regulation, so it can be helpful to have some tools to grab when your amygdala is going haywire.

Do you remember reading the children's book *"The Little Engine That Could"*? (If you haven't read it, get it!) This was a classic, a beautifully simple example of how one little mantra helped one little engine overcome one *big* hill. The little engine constantly repeated, "I think I can, I think I can, I think I can…." And he did. Behavioral researchers Arch & Craske (2006) found that repeating calming or empowering phrases (e.g., "I have done hard things before") can reduce anxiety and improve focus, both of which are critical for career motivation. Your mantra should be something you can relate to and retrieve quickly. Some examples may be:

"Keep on keeping on."

"It is what it is."

"This too shall pass."

"I've got this."

So, what will be your mantra? You may already have one, and if so, I want you to call upon it and say it each time you feel a surge of high stress or worry. What's great is that you don't need anything for this strategy; you only need a few seconds to say it and let it sink in. Say it a few times if you need to - that's just more input for your brain to calm your body down. With practice, our mantras transition from conscious efforts to automatic cues, forming habitual mental frameworks that guide our behavior and enhance our perseverance. In a nutshell, they help us up our own big hills.

What's your mantra?

_____

_____

_____

_____

_____

_____

_____

_____

_____

_____

_____

_____

_____

_____

_____

_____

_____

_____

_____

Chapter 11

Visual Beauty in Your Space

———————•———————

I want you to think of your desk (or your rolling cart, if you're a traveling teacher!): what do you see when you walk over to it? Now think about when you sit down (which I know is rare!): what do you see around you as you sit? If your answer is paperwork, clutter, and overall chaos, it's time for a visual makeover!

When I first started writing this book, I was pumped up. I loved to write (hence my English degree) and needed to share these tools with the world to help recruit and retain good educators and leaders. For about three days in a row, I would go into my home office and sit down to write. I had my comfy chair, soft lighting, and a beautiful cup of coffee...and I had a pile of papers, teacher books, pens, highlighters, half-written sticky notes, and even dog toys surrounding me. I had small open containers of manipulatives, visuals, and fidgets all over my desk for easy retrieval when I was teacher-training online, and my office was a hot mess. As I sat in my chair, surrounded by clutter, I found that I could only focus on my writing for a few minutes before my eyes would wander to my pile of papers, prompting me to look through them. Then I'd discover a buried paper with a to-do list on it, so I'd review it and think, "I probably need to get this one thing done now." I would do that one thing, then another, then another, then I'd feel overwhelmed with the stack of to-dos that weren't getting smaller. To be completely transparent, I stopped writing altogether for a few months. My initial motivation had quietly vanished, as if someone had blown out the fire on my matchstick.

Now, don't get me wrong, I was never - and will never be - a super-organized person. I wasn't born with that gene, and I'll happily outsource decluttering to those who are gifted in that area. However, as I thought I had lost my motivation to write, I realized that it wasn't the writing that was unmotivating, but rather my writing space. I dreaded going into my home office because it represented a thousand other tasks that I did as a self-employed educational contractor. I associated my work area with invoicing, writing reports, and creating training slides, as well as numerous phone calls and emails that I could never seem to catch up on. And it was physically a chaotic mess. I knew I had to recapture my motivation to write, but whenever I tried to declutter my writing space, it was short-lived.

Finally, I took my own advice and started watching videos and listening to podcasts about decluttering my office, which ironically led me down the research rabbit hole of how visual surroundings have a significant impact on our day-to-day lives, both at work and at home. Our visual space contributes to our overall mental motivation. Working in a cluttered environment has been shown to increase cognitive load and diminish focus. Research from McMains & Kastner at Princeton University (2011) explains that cluttered environments compete for your brain's attention, leading to cognitive overload and reduced ability to focus on tasks. I am living proof! The good news is that numerous evidence-based studies support the idea that aesthetically pleasing workspaces are associated with higher intrinsic motivation, greater creativity, and more positive emotions. Digging deeper, if your work area can have this strong of a positive effect on *you*, think about how it could affect your students.

So, how do you start? First, try using labeled bins and folders for your "stacks", and put them in a different area off your desk. I kept it simple because I'm not intrinsically motivated to declutter, so I had three bins: file, pack, and toss. This may be a stereotype, but in my 30-plus years of experience, teachers tend to hold onto materials longer than in other careers. Even after that book in your classroom lending library has experienced soda spills, torn corners, and too much pre-teen body spray, you keep it. This probably comes from our exposure to dwindling budgets and lessening access to resources. When I was going through materials and paper clutter, I found numerous research articles dating back over 25 years to when I was working on my first Master's degree. Printed. Stapled. Poorly copied. All of which can now be found electronically in the research archives. Why was I holding on to this? The research itself was now antiquated. Knowing myself, I think I wanted to hold onto a visual representation of all of my hard work at that time. Yet, ironically, this visual representation was one of the very elements working against my current work focus. That irony was enough to encourage me to let it go, toss it, and move on.

After decluttering what you can, which is the not-so-fun part, we can focus on the fun part: gathering aesthetically pleasing materials. What would you love to see when you step into your classroom or office? What brings you joy just by glancing at it? One of the three primary areas of self-determination is autonomy, and aside from any required materials you may have to post or reference in your teaching space, you have the autonomy to select your colors, your theme, your photos that generate joy, and yes even your favorite color of sticky notes!

Surrounding yourself with visually pleasing items doesn't just have a mental effect on your motivation; it has an emotional impact. Simply having beauty in your environment can trigger the release of dopamine, which in turn enhances your mood and encourages productive behavior toward tasks. I told you I wouldn't give you difficult things to do! Creating beauty or energy in your space is fun as well as rewarding. Still, as simple as this concept sounds, you will be amazed at how your career productivity and mood improve after implementing these simple recommendations. Think about the visuals you already have on your walls, desk, or in your classroom, and consider what you are emotionally drawn to. Then, ensure you have clear visibility of them each day. Here are some ideas to jog your memory and prompt you to "picture place" for daily viewing:

Personal / family / student photos:

_____

_____

_____

Homemade cards or hand-drawn pictures from students:

_____

_____

_____

Favorite colors, animals, or patterns:

_____

_____

Posters, pictures, or other wall decorations:

_____

_____

_____

Plants, flowers (real or fake):

_____

_____

_____

Figurines, gifts, or other decor:

_____

_____

_____

Surround yourself with photos, colors, pictures, and sayings that bring you joy and motivation. For example, as a breast cancer survivor, I am drawn to the color pink. If you were to meet me, you would see that my smartphone is pink, my iPad cover is pink, my wallet is pink, and sometimes my purse is pink. My home office is a soothing mixture of soft rose-gold and calming grey, and I have fuzzy pink pillows and a soft-pink throw on my work couch (which is often where you will find my four-legged canine "coworkers"). My office has a bulletin board immediately above my monitor that is filled with beautiful thank-you cards, photos of myself with school district staff who have hired me to speak, motivational sticky notes, and spontaneous (and usually goofy!) family pictures. It's all organized in one visual area that I can see as soon as I sit down. Whenever I'm working from home, I make a point of looking up at this bulletin board and taking a minute to process it all. My space brings me happiness, and when I'm happy, I'm motivated to achieve my goals. I always feel incredibly thankful when I scan the items around me, which can be particularly helpful during stressful moments. Simply taking 1-2 minutes to visually absorb written or photographic images that have brought you joy can be a form of mindfulness that supports your "mind full." So class, your homework will be to surround your workspace with things that bring you joy, and then take purposeful minutes each day to soak up that joy and visually induce that dopamine!

Chapter 13

Motivational posters

---•---

Although we have just covered different aspects of visual beauty and motivation in your workspace, motivational posters warrant their own spotlight. Why? Because in all my years of education, every campus I've ever been on has had some motivational sign in the front office, in hallways, or teachers' classrooms. Now, you may think this is not a big deal - it's the status quo for campuses - but it's very purposeful. The problem that we have, though, is that because these posters stay up year after year, we tend to ignore them. It's not that we don't like them; they have just become part of the wall, like the paint color in the background. We no longer think about the message because we're so busy with other things.

Have you noticed that several years ago, we used to go out shopping for landscapes, florals, or other pictures for our dwelling space and hang them up to decorate our areas? Now, if you go out shopping for wall decor, you may find some landscapes, some florals, or some historical landmarks, but you also find a lot of words. Words on canvas, words that are framed, words to hang up. When did we start buying pictures of just words?? And boy am I guilty of this. When my husband and I were pregnant with our daughter, I found a beautiful, soft, cream-colored wooden hanging sign with the words "Baby's Room" written in baby pink cursive. I had to have it, and I hung it on her door. There was no logic in this - everyone knew where the baby's room was in our house by the constant giggling (or sometimes squealing) that came from the room. The furniture was obviously for a baby's room, with a crib, changing table, and rocking chair in the corner. The door was rarely closed unless we had guests and the baby was sleeping. And if someone needed more evidence to guide them to the baby's room, there were times when an unpleasant smell would linger down the hall during changings (and believe me, it was not hard to find!). All of these elements were evidence, yet I was compelled to hang this sign up because it evoked a feeling in me when I first bought it. I was a new mom, and every time I walked by that door, I could glance at that sign and smile to myself. I experienced pure joy from just two words on a wooden sign. After a few months, though, I stopped glancing at the sign every moment. I still loved it, but I had forgotten about it. Eventually, I packed it away with some of my daughter's 9-to-12-month clothes, but not before tracing the letters with my finger and reading it one more time.

When we come across items featuring inspirational quotes such as signs, mugs, or posters, we're drawn to the words because they resonate with us. We don't buy wooden signs in stores that say, "Better Luck Next

Time", right? We buy words like "Live, Laugh, Love" or "Dream Big." We tend to gravitate towards something positive that makes us feel good. Remember, a key element in self-determination is relatedness. When we relate to the people and things around us, it drives our motivation to continue to be there, to be present. In our schools, we often purchase motivational posters that we hope will inspire the same positive emotions in our students. We strive to create a campus culture of welcoming positivity, a place where students look forward to coming to school instead of dreading it. This has become increasingly critical as we continue to see a national decline in student motivation to attend school, participate in learning, and complete their education.

If you're reading this book at your campus or office right now, I want you to 1) put your book down for just a moment and 2) look around your space. Find something inspiring that you may have bought for yourself or your workspace. Found something? Now fix your eyes on it. Read it to yourself. Now read it out loud. Did reading it or seeing it again evoke any positive feelings? Did reading it remind you of your initial thoughts when you first purchased or received it? If it did, then I want you to start practicing a daily conscious act that will only take seconds each day. I want you to walk into your space each morning, pause, and read that poster. Read that wooden sign on your desk or bookshelf. Read those words, breathe in and out, and *then* start your day. If you're a teacher, start practicing this daily act with your students too! These seconds you give yourself not only put you in a more positive mindset, but they're also a quick way to incorporate a daily mindfulness ritual for your student community, too.

One more thing… if you read something in your space and it has no effect on you (or your students) anymore, consider removing it and finding something else. Look around and see what you gravitate to, what you relate to. Yes, I'm permitting you to shop.

Chapter 14

The Dream Board

———————•———————

When our daughter started Kindergarten, we were living in the same school district where I worked. We had purposely chosen to move to her elementary school's attendance area. We chose the area because of the school's strong leadership, low teacher turnover, and favorable climate. The campus was part of the Franklin Covey educational program, *The Leader in Me*, and students participated in multiple activities throughout the school year to foster leadership and a growth mindset (https://franklincovey.education/the-leader-in-me). One of the principles of *The Leader in Me* was to "begin with the end in mind." One particular campus-wide activity her school held each fall to foster this principle was called "Dream Board Night." As working parents of an only child, my husband and I tried to attend everything offered in the evening. With eager anticipation, we participated in this night without really knowing what it was about. As we entered the cafeteria, we saw tables filled with magazines, old books, posters, shopping catalogs, and a variety of supplies such as scissors, glue, and white poster board. Hundreds of families had shown up for the annual

"Dream Board Night", along with most of the campus staff and their own families. Many students were already busy, diligently cutting out various pictures or drawing on their poster boards. My daughter's principal came over to greet us and explained the purpose of the night: to encourage each student to think about their dreams, then find pictures and post them visually on their dream board. Dreams were limitless, ranging from future careers and dream homes to travel destinations, and whether they envisioned giving back through charity, having a family, or owning pets. As we scanned the tables, we saw students drawing pictures of awards, trophies, and other accolades they hoped to receive. One student had giant cut-out-colored rings strategically placed in the center of his board - the symbol of the Olympics. One thing in common with every board, though, was the excitement and positivity that each student seemed to radiate. There was such an energy, an optimism, a motivational presence in the air. Students could manifest their dreams through this visual representation, and it was like a fire was lit under them.

After the students completed their dream boards, they were hung up and displayed along the hallways of each grade level for the next several weeks. When the students were allowed to take them home, their teachers encouraged them to keep them in their rooms to remain a visual reminder of the possibilities they could attain. Remember in an earlier section how I stressed that mental imagery encourages some of the same neural pathways as actual performance, serving as almost a "rehearsal" for our brain? The same is true for physical imagery. Visual cues like inspirational images or vision boards can also trigger this mental rehearsal effect, keeping desired outcomes (aka dreams) salient and emotionally engaging.

Now apply this research to your own life: what do *you* still dream about? What do you still want out of your career, life, and future? You might be an adult, but you're not finished yet. You're not done dreaming. Whether you're 25 or 75, your dreams still matter. Look back at your "mindset then skill set" section, where you wrote down what you still want out of your career. Now expand those wants into dreams. Another piece of your motivation homework is to create your dream board. My daughter attended her elementary school from kindergarten through 5th grade, and each year we participated in "Dream Board Night." It was extraordinary to see how her dreams evolved. After she went to middle school, my husband and I realized how much we had missed participating in this annual tradition, so we started our own. Each year, typically on New Year's Eve or New Year's Day, the three of us gather around the dining room table to create our dream boards, which we hang in our bedrooms for the year. It doesn't matter if it clashes with my bedroom decor—it's precisely where it needs to be to serve as a visual reminder of our goals. We have sections for career, education, family, health, professional goals, personal goals, spiritual goals, family dream vacations, and "big dreams." And guess what? Each year, we discover that one of us has either achieved a specific goal or made incredible strides toward one.

Your turn: I want you to gather old magazines, mail circulars, catalogs, markers, pencils, and old books, then schedule a time either by yourself, with your family, or with your department or grade-level team (team-building, anyone?) to create your dream board. Continuing to dream is like stoking your fire of optimism. Get to dreaming, and make it happen.

Chapter 14

The Power of Your "People"

———————•———————

By nature, we have a fundamental human need to feel a sense of belonging. Even if you don't consider yourself a super-social person, we are all biologically wired to want to belong. There's even a whole set of research on this need called *belongingness theory* (Baumeister & Leary, 1995). This theory illustrates what many of us experienced during the COVID-19 pandemic's quarantine years: that we need our "people." This sense of belonging also supports the concept of relatedness in self-determination theory, as it motivates our behaviors, belief systems, and the fulfillment we experience in our lives. Although educators possess superpowers that no other professionals can claim, we can become stronger and more self-determined when we surround ourselves with like-minded individuals (hence the saying "strength in numbers").

You've probably had a job at some point in your life that you didn't like. Maybe you took the job as a teenager because that was all that was available, or you accepted your first teaching role without fully understanding the school environment. We've all been there at one time or another, walking into a job or a set of work activities that we dread. I hope this is not you in your current position, but if it is, keep reading. We're still doing the work, and I'm here to help support that sense of belonging you may be desperately needing right now.

Chapter 15

The Buddy System

———————•———————

When you think of your close friends, do you find that at least one is in the educational field as you are? Maybe more than one? Maybe most of your social circle? Just as we like to surround ourselves with like-minded people in our careers, we tend to form friendships with those who share similar values and interests. The simple act of swapping stories, feeling empathy, or finding the humor in a student situation can strengthen our work motivation. Gallup conducted a significant study through its Gallup Workplace Research in 2017 and again in 2022 following the pandemic that indicated having a close friend at work can enhance one's mental health and well-being. Additional findings demonstrated that workers who had a best friend or close friend in their work environment were:

- More engaged (up to 7x more likely to be engaged)

- More productive and committed to their organization

- More likely to stay with their employer long-term (2017 & revised 2022 Gallup *State of the American Workplace* Report)

These findings suggest that fostering and maintaining strong interpersonal connections at work is not only beneficial for our well-being but also for overall organizational performance (i.e., campus, district).

If you're an educational administrator who sometimes feels like the Lone Ranger - working solo against endless challenges - consider how frequently you collaborate with other administrators in your district or agency. Are there any colleagues who are your go-to people to call when there's a challenge? Who do you reach out to when needing to vent about a challenging situation? Who do you shoot that quick email or text to when something incredible just happened on your campus? Who do you find yourself hanging out with after school, talking about much more than schoolwork? These are your people, just as you are theirs, and each positive relationship contributes to your self-determination.

Chapter 16

Revisiting the
Sticky-Note Strategy

————————•————————

In my first official year of teaching, my principal had a practice of jotting down positive comments and delivering them at random times to various teachers' mailboxes. They were never very lengthy, but boy, did they make a bad day get better. If you were lucky enough to receive a note — usually written on his white notepad with his engraved initials — you would proudly share it with others. If you were me, you would save it on your bulletin board above your teacher's desk. Sometimes, my principal would write a few sentences about a lesson he observed us teaching, or a parent who had praised us. At other times, he would write a phrase like, "I'm glad you're here!" or "You rocked that lesson today!" Because his notes were random and you never knew when you might get one, they seemed that much more special. They were a surprise, as opposed to an obligatory note he felt compelled to write after conducting a walk-through or meeting with you; a small act on the surface, but with a more profound impact of sustaining work motivation throughout the school year.

surface, but with a more profound impact of sustaining work motivation throughout the school year.

In an earlier chapter, I emphasized the power of the sticky note as a visual reminder to us of our "word" or goal, thereby contributing to our daily motivation. Now think about your coworkers and how each of them may experience periods of high stress or a loss of their educational passion. What if you, as one of their "people", could stoke some of that optimistic fire within them? Start by grabbing a sticky note (after reading the earlier sections, I hope you have plenty at your disposal now!) Now think of a coworker and a characteristic or skill that makes them special or unique. Jot it down, put it in their box at school (or in their office), and see what happens. Optimism is contagious!

Chapter 17

Professional Development and Training

———————●———————

Now more than ever, knowledge strengthens our superpowers. Students in recent years have changed from those we may have taught 5 or 10 years ago. Children now have academic and social- emotional needs requiring more individualized attention from teachers. They need access to technology that is tomorrow-based. Our need to continuously grow in our field is not just about keeping up; it's our way of practicing the growth mindset that we strive to instill in our students every day. Professional development not only provides us with the opportunity to grow in our field but also fosters growth in our connections with other educators.

Professional development opportunities are just that: opportunities. These activities align with all three elements of self-determination theory: competence, autonomy, and relatedness. Our brains are wired to crave novelty, to be stimulated. While you may enjoy your routines and habits that bring a sense of calm to your life, there is a distinct difference between gravitating toward habits and falling into a rut. Being in a rut mutes our creativity and causes us to lose interest in our work. When we acquire new skills to refresh our instruction and learn cutting-edge technological practices, we expand our area of expertise. This expansion of knowledge and skills has a direct impact on job motivation, as you can approach teaching or leading with a new perspective, armed with activities that can enhance your daily practices, stimulate your dendrites, and keep you motivated (as well as your students or staff).

How does this area fall into the power of using your people? Let me ask you: when was the last time you attended a training or conference and did NOT network with others? Have you ever participated in staff development without talking with your tablemates or your presenters? I'm betting that your answer is "no". Again, as humans who strive to surround ourselves with like-minded individuals who share similar goals and interests, it's in our nature to network when we are in a large group of such people. Sharing stories, asking questions, and probing opinions all enhance our relatedness to our subject areas, coworkers, and ourselves.

Another critical component of self-determination - autonomy - can be exercised in many cases during our pursuit of training knowledge. Although there are some trainings we cannot avoid (i.e., those mandated by campus or district policies), you may have the opportunity to pursue staff development that aligns with what genuinely excites you or reignites your passion. Think back to when you got a catalog in your mailbox or an email from your district or agency, offering various seminars in different areas. Did you find a title or description that you looked forward to, versus one that you dreaded? Did you find yourself begging for funds to attend something that stoked your fire? If you're reading this and thinking that I'm placing too much emphasis on the impact of training for self-determination and motivation, you'd be right. But it's non-negotiable in these educational times, and when you seek to expand your knowledge, you increase your confidence in your abilities. Exuding confidence in your profession supports retention in that profession; it's as simple yet as evidence-based as that. If funding is an issue (and it often is!), consider seeking out free webinars that may be offered in your district or state. There are also national resources that provide short online sessions for educators interested in a specific topic. Find a YouTube channel, blog, or free online subscription that posts thought-provoking or entertaining content you can relate to (with some research behind it!) Whatever you do, keep learning. Stagnation leads to boredom and burnout, but growth keeps your passion alive.

Time to reflect: When thinking about your subject area, grade level, or leadership style, what are three topics or concentration areas you've been wanting to learn more about? Do you want to learn something new to add to your toolbox, or sharpen your existing skills with enhanced practices? Write down specific areas of interest that you could research for professional development and see what you can pursue for this school year. (HINT: You can look back at your original professional goals from an earlier section and see if anything fits here.)

_____

_____

_____

_____

_____

_____

_____

_____

_____

_____

_____

_____

_____

_____

_____

_____

_____

_____

_____

_____

_____

_____

_____

_____

Chapter 18

The Feel-Better Box

———————————•———————————

The power of your people influencing the satisfaction you experience in your job can far exceed momentary visits to the teacher's lounge or weekly PLC meetings. Recall the earlier chapter where we explored how visuals leave a lasting impression, whereas verbal comments, though supportive, tend to fade more quickly. In the next section, we will delve into project-based learning for your homework. I call this project the "Feel Better Box."

The concept is quite elementary, but its impact can be mighty. Find a simple, tabletop box that can open and close, or create a box that can have an opening. You can purchase something decorative that will beautify your space or use an empty tissue box or small delivery box, decorate it, and place it on your desk. I love this project as a beginning-of-the-school-year activity, but if you're reading this book mid-year, you can still benefit from it. This box will become, as promised, your feel-better box. It will store printed out emails from parents thanking you for something you did for their child, sticky notes that someone left you with positive messages (I told you it was contagious!), drawings or doodling that a student decided to gift you, award certificates or recognitions, or positive affirmations you write to yourself and want to keep. Anything that you receive that fills your cup and makes you smile will be placed in this box. Then, if you're having one of those terrible, horrible, no-good-very-bad days, you're going to 1) sit down at your desk, 2) take a few deep diaphragmatic breaths, and 3) take something out of your box to re-read. Re-feel. Re-energize. Re-inspire.

A few years ago when I was speaking at a state conference for early childhood educators, I was sharing the impactful yet simplistic idea of the "feel better box." A young teacher approached me after the session to thank me for providing her with some new ideas. When I asked her how long she had been teaching, she stated it was only her 2nd year, but she was already exhausted with the number of hours she was putting in, paired with having a very challenging set of parents she was trying to please. She mentioned receiving emails from one parent almost daily. She shared the effort it took each day to respond to each message in a way that satisfied the family and justified her teaching decisions. I could tell she was laser-focused on those daily judgements to the point that it was a struggle to see any of the "good".

Witnessing a second-year teacher emotionally and physically drained after frequent challenging parent interactions is one of many examples that led me to write this book. We're losing too many good educators too quickly to burnout because they haven't developed the coping strategies to rationalize their detachment from the identified source of the burnout. As I continued to talk with this particular teacher, I realized that she was devoting all her energy to this one family and this one student, to the point of neglecting to recognize the good she was doing in her classroom. I didn't have a lot of time with her, but in the short time we visited, I asked her, "What is one thing you're proud of this year? Just think of one thing." She asked, "With this kid?" I quickly responded, "No, in general. With any kid, or with your whole class, or with your team." She thought for a moment and then discussed how she had completed a very intensive summer reading academy that many teachers found challenging. She was excelling in concepts left and right. I coached and probed a little more: "So does this reading academy you attended affect all your students?" As she nodded and told me about the progress she had seen in the students, I asked her to repeat what she had said. She again said, "I've seen so much progress in all of my students."

I echoed back, "All of your students." I gave her homework to create a 'feel-better' box and start it by writing down what she had done: *I attended an intensive summer reading academy, and because of my hard work, I have seen progress in all of my students' reading levels.* I asked her to write it, put it in her box, and bring it out to read later whenever she may need it. To add to the homework, I asked her to start looking through the clutter on her desk or in her email inbox and look for positive comments, emails of thanks, or that reading academy certificate, and start filling up her box. So simple, right? However, the physical act of finding positivity and keeping it retrievable has a visual and emotional effect similar to a dopamine hit on our brain. This tangible strategy helps us when we're so low or frustrated that we can't help ourselves, even with our (albeit non-tangible) mantra.

I told you I wouldn't give you anything too analytical or too complex; self-determination strategies should be user-friendly and straightforward to implement, because consistent implementation is what sustains our motivation. Daily or weekly practices are like exercises to keep our motivational muscles strong. If they're too complicated or too time-consuming, you're not going to be consistent because you're trying to balance so many other things. It's nearly impossible to reignite your fire when you're down to your last match. Don't wait until you reach that breaking point—act early. Utilize your people and outside input from others to help you as soon as you start feeling frustrated.

Chapter 19

Not Your People = Not today!

———————•———————

Growing up in Texas, there were always sayings that were used to respond to various situations. We used responses like "Bless your heart" or "he got a little too big for his britches." If you're not southern, you should know that sometimes these sayings were used to wrap up a conversation and move past it. One of my favorite aunts would often say, "Not today, Satan!" in response to something bad or challenging happening in a given moment. This could be said after experiencing something as big as a pipe bursting in the house or as small as being honked at in the grocery store parking lot. It meant, "not today, bad stuff…. I'm rejecting you." Something about saying it out loud and putting it out into the universe helped the situation, even if a chuckle followed it. So, in this next section, I want you to explore how the coworkers and supervisors around you shape your daily behavior, as well as the behavior of others. I want you to think about who your "people" are and who those are that you inwardly say, "Not today."

The positive influence your people have on your relatedness and competence is powerful in supporting self-determination. We are more motivated to pursue our goals and perform well when we feel connected to those around us. Unfortunately, negative influences can have just as strong an effect on our self-determination. These are the folks that you may encounter at any and every job who you know are NOT your people. These are people (or a person) who will challenge your optimism and question your authenticity. They may try to adopt you into their club of negativity and hope you'll join in a pity party with them. Walk softly, friends, because just as daily practices of gratitude and motivation build up over time to enhance your school year, daily exposures to toxic comments can have residual effects on not just your school year, but on your view of the entire educational field.

There will always be coworkers with whom you may dislike or disagree; this is the nature of humanity and our own personal belief systems. However, coworkers that you try to dodge in the parking lot on the way home who want to talk your ear off about the new curriculum are far different than the coworkers who seem to complain about everything from new leadership to the limited choices in the soda machine. These are the colleagues who, every time you ask a question like, "How's it going?" You never get a "fine" because nothing's fine. Nothing is ever going great, nothing is ever okay, and nothing is ever fair.

Now, if you're cringing back while reading this and wondering, "Is that ME?" I want to reassure you that we all have our moments. Again, though, there is a difference between a moment and a mindset. The truth is, these "Negative Nellies" reached this point through a series of multiple challenges and burnout that they probably couldn't recover from, so it stuck with them. They became entrenched in a fixed mindset, meaning they were so deeply committed to this mentality that they couldn't find a way to break free from it. They didn't have any matches left in their box to strike to keep that fire going at work. And they either didn't (or wouldn't) seek out support to fill their matchbox. These are not inherently bad educators, nor are they inherently bad people; however, they may currently lack the self-determination skills necessary to overcome burnout.

As an educator - administrator - behavior analyst - public speaker (whew!), I have not only had my share of bringer-downer encounters, but I have had too many to reference. As a special education coordinator, I never got the "happy" calls when things were calm, parents were happy, and campus staff had no complaints. I was in a position where I received the tough stuff, so in response to that job requirement, I had plenty of practice each day attempting to resolve conflicts. Within my first month as a district-level administrator, I was already attending leadership coaching seminars, participating in book studies on crucial conversations, and earning certifications in IEP facilitation and conflict resolution. This wasn't all by choice; I had to. I knew as a "Positive Pollyanna" that I could not sustain my motivation (or my disposition) in my new role if I didn't get more training in how to respond to complaints, to "venters", and even to potential lawsuits. More training and coaching equipped me with the skill set to respond proactively, which in turn helped me emotionally and rationally detach from conflicts that I would have otherwise taken personally, and then took home with me, only to stew over the next day. Working with challenging people is just part of being an educator, because unlike businesses, teachers have different parents and guardians every year, on top of any turnover in leadership or teammates. That's a lot of new personalities to adapt to each fall, and by the time you figure out the best tactics for communicating with a negative person, there may be turnover again.

I have studied the art of critical conversations for over 20 years, and I still don't pretend to have all the answers. However, over 20 years of practice have undoubtedly given me an advantage in conflict prevention and resolution, which I am happy to share with you. Before diving in, however, I want you to remember that:

1. Negative people who challenge your optimism were not born this way,

2. Various experiences have shaped these people and their behaviors into what they are now, and

3. You can't change anyone; you can only change how you respond to them.

Even if you can't limit your time with that actual coworker, here are some behavioral tips and coping strategies to limit your exposure to unproductive statements. First, consider the relationship you have with this colleague:

- If you are on the same team/grade level, or if this coworker works directly with you in your classroom (e.g., co-teaching classes or working with paraprofessionals), you can't easily eliminate your interactions with them. Or worse, you don't want to foster a more toxic climate by ignoring or arguing with this person; that would be counterproductive. Instead, try tactics such as redirection to another topic, praising something they did, or placing a sticky note in their box (remember that optimism is contagious, and this may also throw them off guard). Alternatively, find a more neutral commonality between yourselves that takes the spotlight off the work climate. For example, do you both have daughters? Try to redirect a complainer by asking a question about their daughter or sharing a funny anecdote about your child. Laughter is also a tool for optimism in the workplace...it's hard to stay in a bad mood when you're laughing!

- If this colleague is someone under your supervision, balancing a professional supervisory relationship with their pessimism can be a bit more challenging, but it is doable. This is the employee that immediately crosses their arms in passive aggressive defense when you approach them with a "to-do" or a request for a performance improvement, or the less-than-passive verbal reactor that immediately responds to any request with quick comebacks like, "I don't have time for that", "I'm doing too much," or "You don't even know what I go through each day." One technique that can be very effective is to balance in-person compliments with the times you're having to assign them a "to- do". For example, suppose one of your staff members only has email interactions with you when you request that they participate more in an activity or job duty. In that case, they may stew over the email or rush to a sympathetic coworker to read it aloud. If you are needing to put a request in an email (especially for a challenging staff member that you want to have documentation of correct information), try offering a face-to- face within that email such as "We're starting a new task force to improve our parent outreach, and with your strong history of positive parent involvement, I'd like to meet with you briefly and get your input on some ways we can extend these ideas across grade levels." Then when you meet with this staff member, you assign the task force activity by giving this person some autonomy and say-so into the elements vs. giving them a chance to say, "I don't want to do this." Remember, autonomy increases intrinsic motivation and allows people to feel more in control of certain aspects of their job, thereby encouraging greater agreement.

- Another technique to encourage productive responses from staff you may supervise is to make daily connections with them. I know, this sounds too easy. However, this is one of those simple yet powerful strategies that sometimes gets overlooked. Many employees who have negative experiences at work may be lacking in relatedness, a key part of self-determination. Just as research shows that strong student-teacher connections increases attendance and participation at school, similar findings are also observed in teacher-teacher or staff-supervisor relationships. Instead of avoiding these doom-and-gloom individuals like the plague, I encourage you to go out of your way to walk past their classroom and say hello or ask them about a project they're working on (whether professionally or personally). Daily connections also decrease the argument of "you don't even know all I do," people.

- If this is a colleague that you don't see as often, there are ways to deflect your time with them without ignoring them.

Here are some responses if you need to limit the toxicity that may emerge when you are confronted with a less-than-optimistic coworker:

"I was just about to go pick up my kid, but do you want to walk me to my car while we talk?"

"I have an idea for that...let me finish what I'm doing and I can shoot you an email with more details."

"I know you mentioned the new [*staff/principal/teacher/etc*] is having difficulty with keeping up our grade level pace - I wonder if you and I can schedule extra time to meet with them and go through a few ideas to help?" (NOTE: This is a strategy that can be a win-win…either the negative staff member will agree to help the one they are complaining so much about and the conflict gets resolved, or the negative staff member decides that's too much work and stops complaining so much about it!)

The underlying theme in this book is that it takes work to learn, apply, and then consistently maintain motivation, optimism, and self-determination skills. We can't simply stand by and wait for others to hand us the things that bring us fulfillment - or even basic satisfaction - in our careers. This is your work, your needs, and only you can recognize what you may need to get back to contentment. If you find that you have joined the pity party and can't seem to leave, I want to gently remind you that you are reading this book for that very reason. You have recognized that a change has to be made, and the better news is that you are making changes right now as you read! Your motivation to dig deeper and find ways to apply new, novel, or positive strategies is a sign of a growth mindset and moving forward. You're working on it right now, so praise yourself for your initiative. I'm over here clapping for you!

Chapter 20

Tech Support

———————•———————

When you started reading this book, several reasons were identified as burnout triggers for educators, with a lack of resources and diminishing planning time being significant contributors. Our post-pandemic society has provided new and innovative tech tools to help support our work behaviors, but this can be a double-edged sword.

First, let's discuss the benefits of utilizing specific technology to alleviate career anxiety and reduce workload. Teachers often cite administrative workload (grading, attendance, lesson planning) as a significant stressor and time-sucker. Tech tools that automate or streamline these processes can free up valuable time, enabling educators to focus more on direct student interaction, especially in areas like social-emotional learning. SEL is an area that technology cannot (and should not) replace. Virtual meeting platforms have supported educator staff development by providing a "PD in your PJs" way to earn continuing education hours, allowing for knowledge acquisition in the comfort of your own home and minimizing the stress of travelling to a training location.

Research also suggests that technology apps and websites focusing on mindfulness and stress reduction can be beneficial for educators who are burned out. In a recent article published in the *International Journal of Scientific Research in Science and Technology* (http://www.ijsrst.com/), researchers found that mobile and smartphone applications for mental health support can be quite effective, as they allow for self-guidance and promote convenience, accessibility, and quick retrieval of support when needed. Some apps offer mood-tracking options and mindfulness techniques. In contrast, other mobile apps can support therapy needs through text-based or video chats. A great resource is *The Role of Technology in Mental Health: Evaluating Digital Interventions for Psychological Well-being* by Kyndait, Komu, Jamir, Baishya, Kalita, and Das, (November 2024).

These can be helpful tools for stressed-out educators or administrators with busy schedules, challenging student caseloads, and limited substitute teachers on hand.

I'd like you to take a few minutes to recognize your stress level and how it impacts your work performance, sleep, appetite, and social relationships. Keep in mind that although these convenient tech tools can be supportive on a day-to-day basis, they should not be used as a substitute for direct therapy or for more intensive mental health needs.

Always talk with your doctor or PCP to determine your specific level of care needed, and embrace that care to support your sustainability as an educator and as a valuable contributor to the events and people in your life. Remember, mental health is a part of overall health, and helps us be our best selves.

Now, back to that double-edged sword I referenced. Technology support can be a valuable asset in both your personal and professional life. For example, I use *Siri* on my iPhone for voice texting to boost efficiency, and I have recently embraced AI tools to streamline my research process. However, there's no denying the downside: tech fatigue is a real thing, and comes with associated side effects such as reduced human interaction and screen addiction. Tech fatigue is that feeling of being overwhelmed, stressed, or exhausted from using too many digital tools, especially when those tools are complex, constantly changing, or end up adding more work instead of minimizing your workload. It's what happens when technology becomes counterproductive in our lives as we are juggling too many apps, platforms, or tech updates without sufficient support.

Ironically, I asked *ChatGPT* to help me highlight the most common signs of tech fatigue in educators, based on the most current research from 2021 to the present day. After verifying this data (always, *always* confirm any research links and data from any AI, as it can make mistakes!), these were the findings:

Common signs of tech fatigue in teachers:

- Feeling mentally drained after using multiple platforms daily

- Frustration with constant logins, glitches, or tech troubleshooting

- Losing time to learning new tools rather than focusing on students

- Reduced motivation or energy to try new digital tools

Using *ChatGPT* AI is an example of tech support being helpful in my writing workload, as it decreases my search-for-research time. However, my practice of spending over an hour on my matching-game or word puzzle apps while my laundry sits in the dryer (forgotten, wrinkling as the time goes by) is an excellent example of tech overload and non-productivity. I've tried justifying this time as my personal self-care time, but so far it's not flying with anyone! Don't get me wrong, I'm not asking you to stop your gaming apps if that's your down time – I love to pass my airport time that way – but limit and balance productive tech vs. non-productive or overwhelming tech. So, in summary, find tech supports that help you and your motivation to teach, lead, or learn…not those that add to your plate of to-dos.

Chapter 21

Outsource What
You Can, When You Can

———————●———————

When I was first diagnosed with breast cancer, I was so overwhelmed with my medical to-do list and trying to cover work responsibilities that I didn't stop to think about all of my Mommy duties, housekeeping duties, my role as a wife, and my many other lives outside of my work. Things were happening so fast my head was spinning. Within two short weeks, I was diagnosed, staged, had a medi-port surgically put in, and was about to start my first of a 6-month round of aggressive chemotherapy. My aunt (my mother's sister) had gone through her first cancer diagnosis in her 30s as well, and my aunt told my mother that the best support she received during her own chemo was her mother-in-law paying for a housekeeper to do the heavy-duty work. So my mother, living 3 hours away, told me that during my chemo she was going to "gift" me the services of a housekeeper to come once a month for deep cleaning. I happily, yet humbly, accepted this gift and soon discovered what tremendous support it was.

Enter Hilda: a no-nonsense, quick-working lady who seemed to accomplish things in half the time I was able to do them (even before chemo!). As weeks went by, my energy diminished, and my motivation to do chores was low. I was still working full-time and was barely able to sustain my schedule. Any energy I had left at the end of my workday was given to our baby girl, who wasn't even crawling yet. Knowing that I didn't have to get on my hands and knees to scrub the shower tile was a massive weight off my shoulders. Instead, I could use whatever energy I had to get on my hands and knees to have tummy-play with our daughter. Each time Hilda came, the house smelled wonderful. I felt content. I felt happy. My husband could focus his energy on me and our baby. Hilda knew our situation and would do little things like fold baby blankets into cute shapes and leave them in the crib, or organize my multiple bottles of pills on my bedside table into an order that made complete sense. I began hugging her and tearing up each month when she left, so incredibly thankful that we could outsource this need so we could focus on other areas.

You don't have to have a serious illness to seek out or accept help. Instead, recognize the parts of your personal life that are draining your motivation and affecting your work. Then, consider outsourcing. Are you spending hours on the weekend grading papers or prepping IEP documents, only to mow the lawn in your minimal spare time? Are you working with challenging students at school and then facing your own child's behavioral challenges at home? What area(s) could you use a little help with? Even an extra hour per month of support, accumulated over time, can make a significant difference when considering each school year. Emerging research suggests that high job stress contributes to work–family conflict, and that conflict can exacerbate educator burnout. As stated in previous chapters, educator burnout is not just emotional; it's physical. It's the gradual depletion of our energy reserves. Outsourcing home duties may help reclaim some of that lost energy and buffer against work–family conflict.

Unless you love yard work and find it therapeutic, consider hiring a broke high school kid to mow your lawn. Schedule a monthly date with your significant other and arrange for a babysitter for a few hours. Check out a Mother's Day Out program. Hire a professional to paint your bedroom instead of spending a whole weekend on the task. Order out vs. cooking when you're so spent you can't seem to reset before dinner. Consider 1) what are things that, built up over time, wear you out and trickle into your work life, and 2) among those things, what can you afford or consider disseminating to someone else? Who are your people who can join your village? Support from others can be a beautiful thing for your peace of mind.

And in case you were wondering, almost 20 years later, we still have Hilda each month. After chemo was over, we realized her support - physically and emotionally - was something we didn't want to live without. She became a part of our village and ultimately a part of our family.

Your turn: Consider what areas contribute to your lack of energy, and where you may outsource for support.

Things (duties, chores, responsibilities) in my life that challenge and affect my work motivation:

_____

_____

_____

_____

_____

Potential resources or outside supports I can consider:

_____

_____

_____

_____

_____

Follow-up steps/action items:

_____

_____

_____

_____

_____

Chapter 22

The Power of YOU

———————————●———————————

You are unlike anyone else. The gifts you bring to your career are immeasurable, yet at times, you may underestimate the power you hold over your habits, behaviors, and the results you achieve. Yet you have the power to determine how you will continue to grow in your educational journey. You have the power to retrieve and use your acquired tools. In this next section, we will delve deeper into the daily practices of mindfulness and self-love. These daily tools, when used in conjunction with our visual strategies and our village of support, will increase in impact the longer you use them.

In his international best-seller *Atomic Habits*, author James Clear believes that to change our identity at work, at home, and in life, we need to practice small, bite-sized habits that will make a substantial impact over time. Clear writes, "Making a choice that is 1 percent better or 1 percent worse seems insignificant in the moment, but throughout moments that make up a lifetime, these choices determine the difference between who you are and who you could be." (Clear, 2012). Applying this principle to the self-determined teacher, implementing self-determination strategies and proactive tools for optimism by just 1% each day will compound over weeks, months, and even years to come. This way of thinking can make all the tools in this book less overwhelming and more doable.

Based on the power that you have to change your mindset and your motivational skill-set, what kind of educator could you be this time next year?

Your turn:

This time next year, I can picture myself …...

_____

_____

_____

_____

_____

_____

_____

_____

_____

_____

_____

_____

Chapter 23

Strategic Self-Love

———————●———————

If the past decade has taught us anything, it has stressed the importance of self-love and self-care. We hear it on the news, in magazines, and on podcasts. Following the COVID-19 pandemic, school districts and agencies nationwide began to emphasize self-care to support and retain their educators. Some of you may have heard the term "self-care" until you were absolutely sick of hearing it.

But what does self-love honestly look like? When someone tells you to practice self-care, what comes to mind? When I first started focusing on self-care, I tried the typical working-mom strategies: taking a hot bath, getting a massage, or taking a few minutes on a weekend to read a book for pleasure (I was known for always reading work-related books....yes, for pleasure). However, I soon discovered that these are singular events that are few and far between, rather than actual daily practices and sustainable strategies. The truth was, I tended to wait until I was utterly exhausted to think about getting a massage or taking a hot bath to relax. Then, if I carved out time for that event, the relaxation effects were fleeting and brief at best. Sounds like you, too? This is entirely counterproductive to supporting how we should care for ourselves.

Let's revisit the beautiful car analogy from the earlier chapter, *Recognizing Your Burnout*. You love that car - it's gorgeous. It's *you*. When the engine stopped working, you took action and chose to have it repaired. Now, visualize yourself taking it with you on a long journey, and halfway down the path, you see that you're running low on gas. Do you wait till you can go as far as you can until you are out of gas completely, coasting on fumes into the gas station with your "E" light angrily blaring at you? (And I'm not counting what we did in high school or college to get by!) Or, knowing you have miles and miles ahead of you, you fill up before you get totally on "E"? Taking the analogy further, when you do finally stop to get gas, would you buy just a couple of gallons to move your gas gauge a little, only to find that you can't go very far without having to stop and fill up again? And then again? And by this time, you're exhausted from the constant stops you have to make and the time you're losing on your journey, so frustration begins to build. Again, outside of our teenage habits, we wouldn't run our tank down to empty and then add just a couple of dollars' worth of gas, not knowing how soon the next gas station may be available. We fill up when we can with the reassurance that we can go longer, go further.

My biggest problem as an educator was that I would wait until I was completely out of gas (energy), hot and tired, before pushing my hypothetical car into the gas station and taking some action to try to fill up again. Then, my feeble attempt to take a bubble bath or read for pleasure would partially refuel me, albeit temporarily, only to last for the rest of that day. Then I would return to the stress that was causing me to burn out, and so on and so on. This kind of "go till you drop" thinking is unsustainable for our motivation and daily optimistic habits, and it's detrimental to our mental and physical health. Yet somehow, I had been wired to believe that this way of thinking was the key to getting ahead and staying ahead. Keep going, keep running, keep moving until you have nothing left to give; that's when you'll feel success. Instead, it was the primary way to burn out faster.

Let's do a quick pulse check:

1. Do you have ways to reset and refuel your energy before you get to an emotional "empty tank"?   Yes / No

2. Do you have at least one daily activity or practice that you use at work to keep your energy and motivation up? Yes / No

3. Do you do one thing each day that is just for yourself, that has nothing to do with work? Yes / No

4. Do you have a regular stress outlet, such as exercise, a sport, an outdoor activity, a hobby, mindfulness or meditation practices, religion, or therapy support? Yes / No

5. On average, do you get an adequate amount of sleep? Yes / No

Now count up how many Yes's you had: _____

How many No's you had: _____

This may be an eye-opener to you, and my hope is that some of your "no's" may guide you to creating your short-term daily goals and habits. Although education is an extremely stressful profession, and no one can be perfect, if you counted more than two "no's" in your pulse check, it's time to do a little more work. Remember, small steps lead to big gains, and I want you to focus on the process and not just the product. Again, I promise, you're worth the work. No one can do what you do!

Chapter 24

Diaphragmatic Breathing

———————•———————

Where are my science teachers? PE coaches? Choir directors? Swim team? These individuals can describe to you precisely what diaphragmatic breathing looks like and the differences between the typical, short breaths we tend to take and the deeper breaths that come from the diaphragm. Diaphragmatic breathing is a powerful, evidence- based technique for calming the nervous system and reducing immediate stress. This matters because stress and motivation are inadvertently related. Deci & Ryan's research on *Self-Determination Theory* (SDT) shows that stress blocks the three core motivators: autonomy, competence, and relatedness. High stress undermines our intrinsic motivation by reducing energy, focus, and job satisfaction. However, the simple act of practicing diaphragmatic breathing helps us become more aware of physical stress signals and become more able to calm them. Over time, consistent practice trains the nervous system to recover more quickly from emotional or physical stressors. It reduces the intensity and duration of the stress response. (Hopper et al. 2019, *Journal of Psychiatric Research*).

So, what does diaphragmatic breathing look like and feel like? These are deep, slow "belly" breaths that expand your stomach out on the inhale (vs. the exhale) and activate the parasympathetic nervous system. Try this:

1. Sit in a chair (or lie down comfortably if you're practicing at home).

2. Place one hand on your chest and the other on your belly.

3. Inhale deeply through your nose, allowing your belly to expand and rise more than your chest.

4. Exhale slowly through the mouth or nose, feeling your belly deflate.

5. Repeat for 1–3 minutes, focusing only on the breath. Try not to think of anything else except your breath in that moment.

This practice may take a few tries to perfect. Still, once you master this technique, you can use it in various ways throughout your day. Think about accessing this breathing when you're about to walk into a challenging meeting, when you have to make a tough phone call to a parent, or when you are dealing with a demanding student who is trying your patience. In turn, you can teach your students how to apply this practice to manage their stressors and help them develop their own self-regulation.

Chapter 25

Micro-Mindfulness Activities

———————•———————

Y ou have probably heard about the practice of mindfulness, which involves being present in the moment and accepting openness. Mindfulness teaches us to focus on the present, fully experiencing and appreciating what is happening around us. You may have watched videos on the practice or even downloaded an app to your phone. You may have had training or read books on the benefits of incorporating mindfulness practices with your students in class, especially given the increase in technology addiction, trauma, and childhood stress. Mindfulness is a powerful, research-backed strategy that remains significantly underutilized in education, yet it can be introduced with just a few intentional minutes each day. There is a great website that I've referenced in some of my trainings, Edutopia.org, that is chock-full of beneficial articles and evidence-based practices for educators. In a blog from their site titled *Integrating Mindfulness in Your Classroom Curriculum* (Shardlow, 2015), the author reiterates the benefits of using Mindfulness for both students and staff:

Imagine if, along with giving our children the gift of lifelong learning and the tools to become kind and productive adults, we could also give them the gift of Mindfulness -- using their breath and mind to lead a happy and healthy life. In turn, teachers will reap the benefits of Mindfulness as well; we all know that a happy teacher has a happy classroom. https://www.edutopia.org/blog/integrating-mindfulness-in-classroom-curriculum-giselle-shardlow

So, what does this look like for a busy teacher who barely has time to pee, or a juggling-jobs administrator who is in ten places at once? Micro-mindfulness! We can trace some aspects of this type of mindfulness back to Dr. Jon Kabat-Zinn, a microbiologist working at the University of Massachusetts Medical School in Worcester, and the renowned developer of MBSR (*Mindfulness-Based Stress Reduction*). This program teaches how to incorporate mindfulness to decrease stress. Micro-mindfulness strategies are my approach to incorporating 2-3 minutes of mindful activities each day, both as preventative and responsive practices to daily educator stress.

Preventative practices can put your mind in a ready-to-tackle-anything mode, with your body communicating with your brain that you can enter the classroom or office environment calm and centered. Beginning your workday with mindfulness techniques promotes emotional regulation, reduces reactivity, and enhances your brain's capacity to manage stress and challenges. I first began reframing mindfulness practices from something only a yoga guru would do to a secular, day-to-day health practice perspective when I participated in a book study with fellow school district administrators. The book was *Mind Over Moment* (2020) by Anne Grady, an entrepreneur, speaker, and mother of an adult son with autism and mental illness. Being a speaker on autism myself, I was immediately drawn to her story and how she overcame multiple challenges. A now social-media friend of mine and renowned speaker in resiliency, Anne states, "Mindfulness does not require you to sit in a full lotus position, eat tofu, and find your Zen. It is simply being where you are when you're there. This awareness makes you less likely to hit the panic button." (*Mind Over Moment*, A. Grady)

We know that resilience keeps us going, but building initial motivation through self-determination practices gets us started. Go back to our section on visual supports, such as motivational posters or dream boards. As stated, both mental and physical imagery activate some of the same neural pathways as actual performance, allowing you to combine the two supports for micro-mindfulness moments. For example, when you walk into your classroom or office each morning before students arrive, stop at one of your visual supports. Look at your motivational poster or sticky note of self-awesomeness, then take a deep breath in, blow it out slowly, and read your visual twice. You can read it to yourself, but when I tend to read out loud, it resonates a little more with me. And if I read it out loud twice, breathing deeply in between, the second reading always sounds like a more profound sense of conviction. Conviction equals competence, and competence is critical for the self-determined teacher.

Simple, natural micro-mindfulness opportunities may also include taking deep, diaphragmatic breaths in and out when you stand up each morning and place your hand on your heart to recite the pledge. It's a small addition to a daily routine you likely already do on autopilot. Another quick opportunity, if you teach younger students or elementary students, is to take a deep breath immediately when transitioning outside for recess. Don't just walk your students outside and casually monitor; take deep breaths in and be aware of the smell of the grass, the sound of your students laughing, and the feel of the warmth (or cold!) on your cheeks. If you work with older students, consider incorporating diaphragmatic breathing opportunities when walking from one building or hallway to another. You have to transition anyway, so make the most of that time!

Another example is to look at a specific item of beauty you have added to your space and absorb its beauty on a sensory level. If you have a plant in your space, lean in to smell the freshness of the leaves. Breathe in the scent deeply, then exhale it. Put your hands in the soil and feel the natural graininess on your fingertips. (Hint: This also helps you check if you need to water!) Stop and think for a minute about the energy the plant may be exuding, and the visual beauty it brings to your room. If you have a fluffy pillow, walk over to it and brush your hands across the material, feeling the softness and comfort that it provides. Try breathing deeply, then saying your mantra while feeling the soft pillow with your fingertips. Or read something from your feel-better box, then close your eyes and feel how your body, mind, and spirit feel in that moment. This combination of motivational tools works synergistically to support your mood, reduce stress, and foster an attitude of gratitude. And better yet, these preventative practices can be effective even if you only have one minute. A great technique to test this statement is to set your timer or smartphone for 60 seconds, then sit quietly and breathe in and out deeply until the timer goes off. You will be amazed at how long one minute is, yet how effective that time can be.

Expanding on this idea of micro-mindfulness, think about how you may incorporate easy-cheesy weekly practices into your department meetings, co-planning time, or PLCs:

- Pass out sticky notes to each member in the group, then have them write down one positive thing that happened to them that day. After everyone finishes, ask them to take a deep breath in through their nose and out through their mouth, and then take turns reading their positive event (this is a good activity for smaller groups).

- Have staff share out what their visual motivation is in their space and how it helps them each day. Or, have them take a picture of their visual motivation and then share out various examples in a faculty or team meeting.

- If there is a teacher or leader on your campus who is already incorporating mindfulness and using the practice consistently, consider visiting their space and speaking with them one-on-one to learn how they integrate these practices.

• Get large butcher paper or chart paper and post it by the teacher mailboxes or in the staff lounge. Write at the top, "Things I'm grateful for in my job", then leave markers handy so staff can write statements as they pass by the chart. Simply by stopping what we are doing and taking a minute to write a gratitude statement, we engage in a form of micro-mindfulness. This brief act redirects our brain from the stress of calling a parent back during our lunch or reading mail from our box as we rush down the hall to our next class. Bonus: staff can see each other's responses, thus encouraging an environment of optimism and relatedness. Self-determination score!

• Incorporate a brief staff development on mindfulness practices at work and in the classroom, and the research behind its benefits. If you're working with a few negative non-believers, emphasize the benefits that mindfulness has on social-emotional learning for students while encouraging teachers to model these strategies each day. Modeling and practicing these skills daily with students still counts as self-support!

Chapter 26

What's Your Jam?

———————•———————

When I became a district administrator, I oversaw special education practices, compliance, and specialized instruction at multiple campuses. I prided myself on being a boots-to-the-ground, physically present leader who often visited classrooms and collaborated with campus staff. I loved seeing students, hearing teachers report progress, and seeing how I could make a difference. I felt (and still feel) like I'm in a position of service in my career.

However, not every day was unicorns and rainbows...some days were just mentally exhausting. If I encountered a teacher who was having a terrible, horrible, no-good, very-bad day, and I unknowingly happened to ask, "How's it going?" I might get a plethora of complaints in response. As a behavior analyst, I understood there were multiple factors behind that kind of response. But as a person, I often felt helpless, sometimes even defensive. On one occasion, I was talking with a first-year teacher as she was venting about all the behavioral challenges in her room and the paperwork she couldn't keep up with. Everything was "wrong" according to her: her campus mentor was not meeting with her regularly, she had a hitter/kicker kiddo in her classroom, and she claimed she never got support from her campus administration. She definitely had legitimate reasons to complain, so by the time I visited her classroom to offer support, she was guarded. She looked at me and said, "Nothing you can offer at this point will help. I'm just done." Now I had heard tons of teachers in my career say that statement, "I'm done", but typically it was just a bad day and they needed a major reset, support, and some more resources. But this teacher sounded different, and I was genuinely concerned that she would leave at the end of the year and never return to teaching.

I was wrong.

She left at the end of the week.

I was sitting in my car when I received a call from the principal, who informed me that his teacher had resigned with just a couple of days' notice. The principal knew it was a high-needs classroom and asked me how we were going to find a replacement teacher mid-year, given the existing shortage. After we agreed to review the teacher application pool and debrief in a couple days, I hung up and continued to sit in my car, not moving. I had already had a tough week myself, and this was another layer of stress. I worried about this teacher, I worried about her students, and I knew that the principal would be getting tough calls from parents in the classroom. And if the parents didn't get the answers they wanted, they would call me next.

I felt like I couldn't drive, like I couldn't concentrate. I questioned if I could have done more. I felt defeated. Once again, my behavior analyst brain stepped in, reminding me that this was just one challenging situation stacked on top of others from the week. *This too shall pass*, my brain whispered, but I ignored that voice. I sat in silence for I don't know how long before realizing it was a Friday afternoon and everyone had gone home for the weekend. The parking lot at the campus I was leaving that day was empty, a ghost town, and I realized how long I had been sitting there in the quiet.

Reluctantly, I turned the key to start my car, and I jumped at the loud volume I had on my radio. I had been rocking out earlier that day; music was my love language and my radio was always on in my car. As I reached for the volume button to turn it down, I realized the song playing was *"Don't Stop Believing'"* by Journey (Columbia Records, 1981). Now, I have heard this song approximately nine thousand times in my life, and when you hear a song that often, you don't think much about it anymore, except for its familiarity. On this day, however, I chose to keep the volume up and continued sitting in my car, listening to the words. Then I started singing the words. Then I started shout-singing the words (yes, there may have been some neighborhood dogs barking in response). I had loved singing since I was little and it was something that I did daily, typically in the shower or occasionally having a "car concert". Music was always present in our home, whether it was my daughter or I singing in the kitchen, my husband playing his playlist while working, or our family belting out a tune together in the car.

Today was different, though; it wasn't just the joy of singing. It was the loud, pulsing volume, the familiar rhythm, and the lyrics. The refrain *Don't Stop Believin'* began to shift my mindset into something more hopeful. My tension left, if only for a few minutes, and I started to feel more reassured. I felt like I could separate a bad situation from my heart and focus on the good things that had happened that week. All of this emotional shift from a song, you ask? Yep. A song. The exact song that I needed at the exact time I needed it.

I later discovered that the writer of *"Don't Stop Believin'"*, Journey's keyboardist Jonathan Cain, wrote the song when everything seemed to be challenging in his life. He and his long-time girlfriend had broken up, his dog had been in a car accident (and had lived, although badly hurt), he was running low on money, and he was starting to question his dream of making it in the music world. Cain called his father to borrow some money, and when he told his father about his self-doubt, his father replied, "We've always had a vision, son. Don't stop believing." Enter optimism. When Cain's motivation was at its lowest, he dug deep and wrote one of the most popular and most downloaded songs of all time. Cain himself stated, "I believe this song is about wanting to make it," he said. "Where you think you're stuck in life — that you're able to get out, the same way I got out" (Source: NPR article, *Don't Stop Believing' Goes on and On, Because We Need It To*, Roben Farzad, September 2019)

Everybody has that one song that can change your emotional stress in 3 minutes (or less) if you stop, focus, and listen to it. True, a song can't fix a challenging situation, but it can alter your immediate mindset. It helps you reframe a challenge, even if only for a few minutes. This is another easy idea for your micro-mindfulness toolbox.

For years, I have included an exercise in one of my staff development training sessions in which I ask participants to take a few minutes to find that *one* song, the song that always resonates with them and causes a shift in their thinking. Over the years, I've gotten answers that include rock songs, heavy metal songs, religious or spiritual songs, country songs, rap songs...even songs I've never heard of from artists I've never heard of. My husband calls me the "walking jukebox" because of my love for all genres of music. If a participant mentions a song I don't know (which humbly speaking is rare), I'll look it up and play it during the next break. I love hearing why a person chooses a particular song and how it makes them feel when they listen to it. It's also a gift when I can add new songs to my playlist of motivational music for days when just one song doesn't quite cut it.

Your turn: So, what's your song? Your jam? Your rhythmic motivation? It could be slow and soothing or loud and proud. Take a minute to think about it, and write it down:

_____

_____

_____

_____

_____

_____

_____

_____

_____

For days when you need a little more inspiration, such as the drive to work on a tough morning or the drive home after a long day, what will you include in your motivational playlist? Write your runner-ups and download them to have handy whenever you need a rhythmic boost:

_____

_____

_____

_____

_____

_____

_____

_____

_____

_____

Chapter 27

Feed Your Basic Need

———————•———————

It's challenging to practice self-care and self-love strategies if you're not attending to your basic needs, which support your body's functioning and brain health. Let's start with your sleep. If your first response is, "What sleep? What's that?" then you might need a little help! Sleep is essential for our job, for our executive functioning skills, our social skills, and our ability to be our best selves. If this basic need is not being met consistently, try some of these simple strategies for at least 3-4 weeks to see if they make a difference:

1. Make your bedroom slightly cooler; the research shows that a cool space can help induce sleepiness.

2. Try to make your sleep space as dark as possible to encourage REM sleep. If this is challenging for whatever reason, try using a sleep mask.

3. Soothing scents, such as lavender and chamomile, can have a calming effect on the body through our sense of smell.

4. Set a timer at night and commit to shutting off the TV, stopping work, or putting away your tech (unless you're reading!) at least 30 minutes earlier than you typically do. Then, crawl into bed after the timer goes off.

5. If you can't shake the screen time before you go to bed (e.g., you read on your tablet or look at your phone), still set a timer and when it goes off, lower the backlight (screen light) on your device to reduce visual stimulation.

6. You work hard! Invest in some new pillows, comfy sheets, or other bedding that supports your relaxation. Yep, another permission from me to shop.

7. Finally, the daily practice of micro-mindfulness, spread across moments throughout the day, helps you stay in a calmer state. Thus, you could have more tranquil, less stressful evenings that support your transition to rest.

Chapter 28

Feed Your Mind

———————•———————

F ood. This is a tough one for some of us (including me), as our food choices as educators tend to be primarily influenced by our daily schedules. When I taught an early childhood autism class at an elementary school, I was often lucky to get out the front door in time for morning bus duty, chugging coffee and snacking on dry cereal from a plastic cup. My students arrived early and had breakfast at school, so at times I would buy a breakfast sandwich or hash brown patty in the cafeteria and eat with them. After our class circle time, I would begin my routine of sipping at least one or two Diet Cokes throughout the day. Lunch was either a quick microwave meal or lunch was non-existent. The kids' afternoon snack time was also snacking time for me, and I often munched on chips or granola bars to keep my energy up (and to keep up with my kids, who were never at a loss for energy!). If it were an exceptionally tough day, I'd drink Diet Coke #3 in the car on the way home. After I would get home from work, I attempted to make a decent meal for dinner; however, if I was exhausted, I had Domino's pizza on speed dial and Sauvignon Blanc chilling in the fridge. Real healthy, right?

I realized that my daily exhaustion was expanding to weekly exhaustion, then monthly exhaustion. I started to realize that when I ate crap, I felt like crap. I also learned that I was a "fatigue feeder"; that is, on days when I was more tired than others, I snacked more throughout the day to try to maintain my energy. It worked temporarily, until I felt my body crashing again and I found myself reaching for another Diet Coke, Snickers bar, or Goldfish cracker pack.

I had always attributed food to a "diet" and wanting to lose weight, so eating healthy meant I must be dieting, and eating like crap meant I was off a diet. This was part of my problem. I had to shift my mindset because my fatigue had nothing to do with whatever popular diet I was on or off, it was simply a matter of eating real meals and real food for fuel vs. processed pseudo-food, snacks, and drinks to feebly fuel me. I started making changes through small behaviors: I didn't (or wouldn't) give up my Diet Cokes completely, but I promised myself that if I were going to drink two a day, I would supplement with water in between the first and second cans and then drive home with a large ice water. I didn't quit snacking cold-turkey, but I substituted carrot sticks and peanut butter, apple slices, and baked chips in place of my poorer choices. I still loved my chocolate, but instead of eating peanut M&Ms on my drive home to keep me awake until dinner, I would buy the "good" chocolate and have a square after a full meal. Was I perfect? Nope. But I was persistent.

If you're an "I can go cold-turkey" person and make overnight healthy substitutions, my hat's off to you. But if change can be hard, consider minor behavioral shifts (remember *Atomic Habits*?) and substitutions versus restrictions. I also want you to shift your vocabulary from "food" to "nutrition." Think about it: the word "nutrition" originates from the Latin word "nutrire," which means "to feed" or "to nourish." When we nourish our body, we also nourish our brain and our emotional needs. Don't expect perfection since I am far from it still, just expect that persistence over time can reap some feel-better rewards.

A simple behavioral strategy to support this shift in thinking is to make a list of your daily drink and food behaviors: not just what you eat and drink, but when you eat and drink, according to your work schedule. Focus on your workdays first, and then you can tackle weekends later. If you're anything like me, my weekends are a time I enjoy a nice dinner, munch on buttered popcorn at the movies, or go out to eat to splurge a little after a tough week. So, focus on your Monday-to-Friday routine to start, since these are typically the days that require more energy from us. Take a moment to write down your weekday eating patterns—from the moment you wake up until bedtime—and then identify any areas you might want to adjust to combat fatigue. Here's an example of a simple template you can use to get started, but feel free to tweak it to work best for you:

Time of day	Activity / Subject	Food / Drink item	Stress level prior to food / drink: (1=low, 2=medium, 3=high	Notes

Please know that this is not a "go on a diet" speech. This is not a diet book, and keep in mind I hate the word "diet" (hence the nourishment vocabulary lesson.) I am not a doctor or related medical professional, and I cannot provide medical advice. When I reference your daily foods, I'm talking about the nourishment you put in your body to perform better physically and mentally. Believe me, my morning cup of coffee helps my mind and body perform better, and I'm not willing to give that up. It makes me happy, and I breathe in the rich aroma of coffee beans each morning as one of my sensory-rich micro-mindfulness moments. If a school principal offers me a small piece of chocolate from his desk jar, you bet I'm going to accept it and savor it. But on a day-to-day basis, I want you to consider the foods that nourish your mind, body, and spirit. You don't have to be perfect, just persistent. Try to recognize what you need throughout the day. You have a precious body that sustains a lot of standing, active monitoring, patience, task juggling, and managing student behaviors. Try to find ways to feed your fire each day, literally.

Chapter 29

The $5-and-Under Rewards System

————————●————————

T he science of behavior tells us that any behavior (good or bad) that is reinforced will be more likely to occur again. This is powerful information for you as an educator of children, but it can be just as powerful when applied to your own behaviors. When you stop and take a step back to realize your day-to-day accomplishments, how do you reward yourself? Or DO you ever reward yourself? For example, the sticky-note strategies and self-love statements are a free and feasible way to intrinsically reinforce your hard work and tolerance. Still, sometimes just a little external reinforcement can be the difference between an "I survived" day and an "I thrived" day.

When I was undergoing chemotherapy, I lost my taste for many foods, such as those with spicy or strong-smelling aromas. Sometimes, even my beloved coffee in the mornings didn't quite taste right. Many times, chemo patients experience a metallic taste in their mouths when eating certain foods or even using silverware, and that was a side effect I unfortunately experienced but tried to overcome. After my second round of chemo, while driving home from the clinic, I suddenly craved a warm, comforting drink. It was a fabulous October day, and I knew that coffee wouldn't sit well with me. We ran through a Starbucks drive-through and I ordered a hot chai tea latte with soy milk (regular milk was *not* my friend at the time!) Although I could smell the cinnamon spice, it did not cause my stomach to turn. Instead, it was quite soothing to me. I sipped it slowly, savoring the light aroma of spice. As we drove home, I felt the stress from my body start to melt away. Money was tight for us with so many medical bills (and we were still paying off our hospital bills from the baby's delivery), and we were being frugal with our expenses, so even a fancy store-bought hot drink felt like a special treat. A couple of weeks later, right after my next chemo treatment, we stopped again for my chai tea latte. This time, it felt like a reward—a special treat for enduring such a challenging task as chemotherapy. Over the years and into my remission, I started making it a practice to reward myself with my chai tea after my 3-month cancer checkups, then my 6-month checkups, and finally my yearly checkups. Now, over 18 years later, I still stop for that chai tea latte after my yearly oncology appointments. It's such a small treat, but it represents the reward of health, strength, and perseverance. Moreover, it's another sensory-rich micro-mindfulness moment that nourishes my spirit.

We all need reinforcement in our lives to continue performing optimally, enduring challenges, and thriving. Reinforcement helps maintain and improve behaviors, regardless of your age or your position.

Think about a time that your principal or other administrator dropped by your room to relay something extraordinary that you did, such as a creative lesson that you taught or a contribution you made to your team. How did you feel? Have you ever received a thoughtful thank-you note in your school mailbox or perhaps a mini treat on your desk as a sign of extrinsic gratitude for something you did or said? These tokens of appreciation or recognition, albeit small, bring us a sense of satisfaction. They tend to validate in their own small way what we are doing and how hard we are working. Even if you are a person who doesn't need recognition, when it is offered, you have to admit it feels nice. Someone else thought of you enough to gift you a small token of esteem or thanks, and that feels pretty darn good.

So, let me ask again, do you reinforce yourself? I'm not talking about the once-every-3-month massage or the yearly vacation that I hope you take. I'm referring to a more frequent yet cost-effective schedule of reinforcement. Don't underestimate the reinforcing power of the $5-and-under tangible, especially when it is immediately followed by a challenge you have overcome. Did your students all pass their benchmarks in the fall? Grab that small token of validation for your hard work. Ace a test you were taking toward another degree? Celebrate your efforts with a simple reinforcing gift to yourself. Try a new approach to teaching a "stale" lesson, and rocked it? Pick up that specialty drink on the way home.

Although educators always deserve more money than they earn, enduring frequent challenges for an entire school year until that August salary raise kicks in may not be sustainable for another whole year. Try spreading the wealth across moments versus months. Tackle small challenges and reinforce yourself with small rewards. Studies show that frequent, immediate rewards after positive behavior are more likely to build lasting habits. Start by making a list of simple, low-cost rewards that make you feel awesome, then keep that list on your phone, fridge, or by your desk at work (sticky notes, anyone?) This is another visual motivation, too! Flair pens, your favorite smoothie, a little picture frame you've been eyeing, new golf balls, a paperback book, renting a just-for-you movie to stream? If you need more ideas, try browsing the $5-and-under bins at your favorite stores and add them to your reward list. Praise yourself and reinforce your self-determination!

Do you have a few ideas in mind for inexpensive reinforcers? Write 'em down!

_____   _____   _____   _____

_____   _____   _____   _____

Chapter 30

Motivation Fosters Motivation

————————•————————

I've discussed the three principles of self-determination - autonomy, competence, and relatedness - throughout this book, and relatedness should be considered when you find yourself questioning your motivation in your current position. Being able to relate to others in your field, on your campus, and within your friend group helps support your burnout through empathy, social support, and a sense of community.

Hearing or reading about others' challenges and how they overcame obstacles similar to those you are facing can strengthen your sense of relatedness. While overseeing autism and low-incidence programs in my school district, I met many families navigating the challenges of raising a student with special needs. These parents loved their child unconditionally, but often felt overwhelmed, uncertain, and isolated. Some of these families were going through the grieving process; others were trying to cope day by day with a child who was physically aggressive or self-injurious. A common thread, though, was when these families could hear success stories from other families that had "been there, done that." Sometimes, parents would share a book with me that was about another family facing a similar challenge. These books, podcasts, and success stories helped motivate other families, thus planting the seed for the next success story.

During my cancer treatments, I often wore scarves on my head if my wig got too itchy or irritating to my scalp. On weekends, if my husband and I went out to the grocery store or to run other errands, I was shocked (but touched) by how many strangers approached me and asked, "Are you a survivor?" or "Are you going through treatment right now?" I was never offended; it was as if they just knew. Each woman that approached me would ask how I was doing, then proceed to tell me about how many years in remission they were, or what their journey was like. Each encounter made me tear up, but lit my optimism up like a rocket: I was seeing and hearing about life after cancer. That there was and IS still life after cancer, and a great life at that. To this day, I pay it forward and approach others when I feel like it will be welcomed, and every single time I receive a thank-you and get a glimpse of that optimism shining in their own eyes. Not once have I gotten a "mind your own business" or negative response. Why? Because not only does the human spirit crave connection and belonging (self-determined relatedness and the belongingness theory), but we also love hearing success stories about similar challenges that were overcome.

Suppose you are an educator or leader facing a personal, health-related, financial, or professional challenge. If you are, I encourage you to seek out and read about others who have faced similar issues. Motivation fosters motivation, especially when we can relate to a fellow human being in a particularly personal way.

Chapter 31

Find Your Fun Again

———————•———————

Is education still fun for you? If you're chuckling to yourself, then I guess that your answer is "no". As you incorporate more of these daily self-determination practices into your work routine, you'll rediscover the joy you once had or retain the joy you still have for this fantastic profession. I've always thought that you have to have a certain sense of humor to work in education!

Self-determination theory and its relationship to motivation are not necessarily about having fun all the time. Instead, the theory reinforces the principle that we are either motivated to do something because a) we love it or find joy in doing it, or b) we may not love it, but we find value in doing it, thus we continue the activity or behavior. For example, I am motivated to eat chocolate because I find joy in doing it, but I am motivated to eat kale and juice vegetables because I find value in doing so. I love my work, so motivation comes easily. But when it comes to filing taxes each year, I don't enjoy the process, especially as a self-employed businesswoman. Still, I do it because it's necessary and adds value to my business.

Think about things that you do outside of work that have nothing to do with the educational field, your school, or your district. What do you participate in that supports your self-determination skills? Are you a soccer mom or dad because you feel obligated, or do you genuinely love it, or at least value it? Do you read books outside of your educational genre, just for pleasure? (Don't count this book, though - this one is your matchbox of motivational fire! Feel free to start looking at your personal library *after* this read...hee hee). Do you carve out at least 15 minutes each day that has nothing to do with your job, and only to do with growing your joy and motivation? What's fun for you? Think books, movies, family outings, hobbies, exercise, or anything else that brings you joy or fulfillment that is just for you:

_____

_____

_____

_____

_____

_____

Now, if you were able to list several things that you enjoy or value but are still struggling with the "I-don't-have-time-for-fun" mentality, let me offer some options that may help:

1. Prioritize your interests and hobbies. If you're like me and find many things enjoyable but have no time for yourself, start with one personal activity to incorporate more of and be consistent with that time.

2. Treat this time - even if it's just 15-20 minutes a day - like an appointment you've booked for yourself. Add it to your calendar and don't cancel on yourself! By scheduling instead of trying to seek out downtimes, you'll prioritize yourself more. Try looking at your daily work schedule, including your getting-ready time, commute, and household duties time, and carve out windows each day that are your fun time.

3. Combine your interests with your schedule whenever possible, such as listening to a fun or interesting podcast while driving to and from work, or sitting down to read a favorite novel as you have your students read silently from their own book choices. Students seem to be less and less interested in physical books as they continue to gravitate toward screen time, so you can model pleasure-reading behavior for your students while giving yourself some time each day to find a few minutes of joy. I love listening to podcasts or audiobooks while driving. Other times, I put on a road-tripping playlist and give myself time to enjoy music that makes me smile (and sometimes dance in the driver's seat).

4. Minimize outside distractions by muting your phone, avoiding social media, or engaging in your time in a quiet space. I'm not gonna lie, y'all, this is a tough one for me, but I continue to work on it. I have been known to leave my phone in another room to decrease my chances of checking it every 5 minutes while I'm trying to engage in downtime. That works better for me than just putting my phone on vibrate, but do what works for you to drown out the noise and gift yourself your time.

Your turn: Think about ways to incorporate more joy and fun into your daily routines, or ways to multi-task by incorporating have-to's with get-to's. Start with one idea:

While I am _____[have-to],

I can _____[get to].

PART III

LIFELONG HABITS

───────●───────

If you take some time to look back on some of the strategies you've acquired from this book and reflect on your answers and your own needs, you will find that there are tons of matches to reignite your fire. These are quick, simple, and purposeful, but they are only as effective as your consistency in using them. Take a few tools that resonate with you the most and seem the most feasible to start with, then put those into place before adding more. What I will continue to stress as we wrap up our time together is that 1) self-determination is work, not automatically given, and 2) small daily practices add up over time. This is true of any profession and any role. The more you practice quick, daily motivational strategies, the more they will become habits and the less you will view them as work.

I hope that in reading this book, you have come full circle in your journey of rediscovering your optimism and self-determination in your educational career. If you already had existing strategies, I hope you've discovered more to add to your matchbox of motivational fire starters.

If your fire was close to ashes by the time you picked up this book, I hope that you rekindled or restarted it from a fresh perspective. If you choose to read this book as part of a book study or team-building activity, I hope you surround yourself with your strategies, your people, and your determination to not only inspire yourself but to inspire others.

There will be moments in your educational career that you may need more "matches" than in previous years. When or if that happens, reach for this resource and know that it's yours and yours alone. Throughout this book, you have self-reflected, identified, and pinpointed where you are and where you still want to be. For those days that you find you are struggling more than others, open this book and look at some of your reflections. If it's easier, keep this book out and visible to remind you of your power. It can be one of your visual strategies!

You have more competence, relatedness, and autonomy than you probably ever thought possible. You are - and can forever be - an optimistic educator, keeping your inspirational fire burning to benefit your job satisfaction, your students, your colleagues, and, most importantly, yourself.

You are the self-determined teacher.

Conclusion

The Fire Within
You Is Still Burning

———————●———————

I f you've made it to this final chapter, let me pause for just a moment and say thank you. Thank you for investing in yourself, for carving out the time to read, reflect, and reignite something within you that may have felt dim, distant, or dangerously close to burning out. The fact that you picked up this book, whether out of curiosity or out of necessity, is a testament to the light that still flickers inside you.

Throughout these pages, I've shared my journey: the missteps, the setbacks, the trials, and the triumphs that shaped the educator I became. But more importantly, I've invited you to take your own journey. I asked you to pause, examine your burnout, define your "why," explore your dreams, and surround yourself with people and practices that nourish your purpose, not deplete it.

This book was never about quick fixes or sugar-coated strategies. It was about intentional practices, daily behaviors, reflective actions, and mindset shifts that can build momentum and motivation over time. Because here's what I've learned through experience and evidence alike: motivation isn't magic. It's a muscle. It's something you stretch, strengthen, and sustain through conscious effort and daily decision-making.

Yes, the system is tough. Yes, some days feel thankless, overwhelming, or just plain exhausting. But somewhere in your classroom, your office, or your school building, there is a student or a team member who looks to you for direction, encouragement, or just a little light. And you still have it in you. You are the spark.

Let me remind you of something important: You are not required to set yourself on fire to keep everyone else warm. Your energy, your joy, your peace, they matter. And protecting those things isn't selfish. It's sustainable leadership. The strongest educators are not the ones who give until there's nothing left; they are the ones who keep their flame kindled so that they can provide to others again day after day.

So, keep your visual supports where you can see them.

Speak your mantra when the noise gets loud.

Hang that motivational poster one more time, but this time, read it aloud and believe it.

Look around your space. Make it beautiful.

And when you start to feel unmotivated again, remember: the matches are already in your hands. The fire is already inside you.

This isn't the end. It's a re-beginning.

Now go light it up.

With purpose,
Anissa Moore

References

Akin-Little, K. A., Eckert, T. L., Lovett, B. J., & Little, S. G. (2004). Extrinsic reinforcement in the classroom: Bribery or best practice. School Psychology Review, 33, 344-362.

Arch, J. J., & Craske, M. G. (2006). Mechanisms of mindfulness: emotion regulation following a focused breathing induction. Behaviour research and therapy, 44(12), 1849–1858.

Bardach, L., & Klassen. R.M. (2021). Teacher motivation and student outcomes:

Searching for the signal. Educational Psychologist. Advance Online Publication. https://doi.org/10.1080/00461520.2021.1991799

Baumeister, R. F., & Leary, M. R. (1995). The need to belong: Desire for interpersonal attachments as a fundamental human motivation. Psychological Bulletin, 117(3), 497–529.

Bieg, S., Backes, S., & Mittag, W. (2011). The role of intrinsic motivation for teaching, teachers' care and autonomy support in students' self-determined motivation. Journal for Educational Research Online, 3, 122–140. [Google Scholar]

Brock, A., & Hundley, H. (2016). The growth mindset coach: A teacher's month-by-month handbook for empowering students to achieve. Berkeley, CA: Ulysses Press.

Cain, J., Perry, S., & Schon, N. (1981). Don't stop believin' [Song]. On Escape. Columbia Records.

Camacho, A., Correia, N., Zaccoletti, S., & Daniel, J. (2021). Anxiety and social support as predictors of student academic motivation during the COVID-19. Frontiers in Psychology, 24, article 644338. https://doi.org/10.3389/fpsyg.2021.644338

Chambers Mack, J., Johnson, A., Jones-Rincon, A., Tsatenawa, V., & Howard, K. (2019). Why do teachers leave? A comprehensive occupational health study evaluating intent-to-quit in public school teachers. Journal of Applied Biobehavioral Research, 24(1), e12160.

Clear, J. (2018). Atomic habits: An easy & proven way to build good habits & break bad ones. New York, NY: Avery.

Das, Priyam Jyoti & Kyndait, Pdiangmon & Jamir, Sungjemrenla & Baishya, Dhiraj & Kalita, Juganta & Komu, Lobsang. (2024). The Role of Technology in Mental Health: Evaluating Digital Interventions for Psychological Well-being. International Journal of Scientific Research in Science and Technology. 11. 366-386.

Deci, E. L., & Ryan, R. M. (1985). Intrinsic motivation and self-determination in human behavior. New York, NY: Plenum Press. [Google Scholar]

Deci, E. L., & Ryan, R. M. (2000). The" what" and" why" of goal pursuits: Human needs and the self-determination of behavior. Psychological Inquiry, 11, 227–268.

Deci, E. L., & Ryan, R. M. (2000). Self-determination theory and the facilitation of intrinsic motivation, social development, and well-being. American Psychologist, Vol. 55(1), pp. 68-78.

Digital Promise. (2021). Learning in the 21st Century: How the American Public, Parents, and Teachers View K-12 Teaching and Learning in the Pandemic. Digital Promise: Washington, D.C.

Domen, J., Hornstra, L., Weijers, D., Van Der Veen, I., & Peetsma, T. (2020). Differentiated need support by teachers: Student-specific provision of autonomy and structure and relations with student motivation. The British journal of educational psychology, 90(2), 403–423. https://doi.org/10.1111/bjep.12302

Dweck, C. S. (2006). Mindset: The new psychology of success. Random House.

Emery, D. W., & Vandenberg, B. (2010). Special education teacher burnout and ACT. International journal of special education, 25(3), 119-131.

Grady, A. (2020, September 3). Mind over moment: Harness the power of resilience. Independently published.

Hayes, S. C., Strosahl, K. D., & Wilson, K. G. (2011). Acceptance and commitment therapy: The process and practice of mindful change. Guilford press.

Hopper, S. I., Murray, S. L., Ferrara, L. R., & Singleton, J. K. (2019). Effectiveness of diaphragmatic breathing for reducing physiological and psychological stress in adults: a quantitative systematic review. JBI database of systematic reviews and implementation reports, 17(9), 1855–1876.

Hornstra, L., Mansfield, C., Van Der Veen, I., Peetsma, T., & Volman, M. (2015). Motivational teacher strategies: The role of beliefs and context. Learning Environments Research, 18, 363–392. 10.1007/s10984-015-9189-y [CrossRef] [Google Scholar]

Hornstra, L., Stroet, K., Van Eijden, E., Goudsblom, J., & Roskamp, C. (2018). Teacher expectation effects on need-supportive teaching, student motivation, and engagement: A self-determination perspective. Educational Research and Evaluation, 24, 324–345. 10.1080/13803611.2018.1550841 [CrossRef] [Google Scholar] https://doi.org/10.1080/13803611.2018.1550841

Hornstra, L., Van Der Veen, I., Peetsma, T., & Volman, M. (2013). Developments in motivation and achievement during primary school: A longitudinal study on group-specific differences. Learning and Individual Differences, 23, 195–204. 10.1016/j.lindif.2012.09.004 [CrossRef] [Google Scholar]

Kabat-Zinn, J. (1990). Full catastrophe living: Using the wisdom of your body and mind to face stress, pain and illness. Delacorte Press.

Keller, J. M. (1987). Development and use of the ARCS model of instructional design. Journal of Instructional Development, 10, 2-10.

Lam, S. F., Cheng, R. W. Y., & Ma, W. Y. (2009). Teacher and student intrinsic motivation in project-based learning. Instructional Science, 37, 565–578. 10.1007/s11251-008-9070-9 [CrossRef] [Google Scholar]

Lin-Siegler, X., Dweck, C. S., & Cohen, G. L. (2016). Instructional interventions that motivate classroom learning. Journal of Educational Psychology, 108(3), 295-299.

Lonsdale, C., Hodge, K., & Rose, E. (2009). Athlete burnout in elite sport: A self-determination perspective. Journal of Sports Sciences, 27, 785-795.

Luketic, R. (2001). *Legally Blonde* [Film]. Metro-Goldwyn-Mayer Distributing Corporation (MGM).

Madigan, D. J., & Kim, L. E. (2021). Does teacher burnout affect students? A systematic review of its association with academic achievement and student-reported outcomes. International journal of educational research, 105, 101714.

McMains, S. A., & Kastner, S. (2011). "Interactions of top-down and bottom-up mechanisms in human visual cortex." Journal of Neuroscience, 31(2), 587-597.

Milne, A. A. (1926). Winnie-the-Pooh. E. P. Dutton.

Niemiec, C. P., & Ryan, R. M. (2009). Autonomy, competence, and relatedness in the classroom: Applying self-determination theory to educational practice. Theory and Research in Education, 7, 133-144.

Paliliunas, D., Burke, R. V., Taylor, S. L., Frizell, C. B., Durbin, K. K., & Hutchings, D. L. (2022). Evaluating an ACT-Based Brief Intervention for

Educators Treatment Package on Reported Well-Being and ACT-Consistent Language in the Classroom. Behavior analysis in practice, 16(1), 156–171.

Parker, D. (2019). Building bridges: engaging students at risk through the power of relationships. Bloomington, IN: Solution Tree Press.

Piper, W. (2001). The little engine that could. G P Putnam's Sons.

Ryan, R. M., & Deci, E. L. (2017). Self-determination theory: Basic psychological needs in motivation, development, and wellness. New York: Guilford.

Saeed, S. & Zyngier, D. (2012). How motivation influences student engagement: A qualitative case study. Journal of Education and Learning, 1 (2), 252-267.

Shardlow, G. (2015, November 18). Integrating mindfulness in your classroom curriculum. Edutopia. https://www.edutopia.org/blog/integrating-mindfulness-in-classroom-curriculum-giselle-shardlow

Skinner, E. A., & Belmont, M. J. (1993). Motivation in the classroom: Reciprocal effects of teacher behavior and student engagement across the school year. Journal of Educational Psychology, 85, 571–581. 10.1037/0022-0663.85.4.571 [CrossRef] [Google Scholar]

Slamecka, N. J., & Graf, P. (1978). The generation effect: Delineation of a phenomenon. Journal of Experimental Psychology: Human Learning and Memory, 4(6), 592–604.

Vansteenkiste, M., Sierens, E., Soenens, B., Luyckx, K., & Lens, W. (2009). Motivational profiles from a self-determination perspective: The quality of motivation matters. Journal of Educational Psychology, 101, 671–688. 10.1037/a0015083 [CrossRef] [Google Scholar]

Wigfield, A., & Eccles, J. S. (2002). Development of achievement motivation. San Diego, USA: Academic Press.

www.ingramcontent.com/pod-product-compliance
Lightning Source LLC
Chambersburg PA
CBHW071308130626
46556CB00004B/1525